A Patriot for Me

AND

A Sense of Detachment

also by John Osborne

plays

THE END OF ME OLD CIGAR and JILL AND JACK
THE ENTERTAINER
THE GIFT OF FRIENDSHIP
INADMISSIBLE EVIDENCE
LOOK BACK IN ANGER
LUTHER
A PLACE CALLING ITSELF ROME
THE RIGHT PROSPECTUS
A SUBJECT OF SCANDAL AND CONCERN
TIME PRESENT and THE HOTEL IN AMSTERDAM
UNDER PLAIN COVER and THE BLOOD OF THE BAMBERGS
VERY LIKE A WHALE
WATCH IT COME DOWN
WEST OF SUEZ
THE WORLD OF PAUL SLICKEY
YOU'RE NOT WATCHING ME, MUMMY
and TRY A LITTLE TENDERNESS

with Anthony Creighton

EPITAPH FOR GEORGE DILLON

adaptations

A BOND HONOURED (from Lope De Vega)
HEDDA GABLER (from Henrik Ibsen)
THE PICTURE OF DORIAN GRAY (from Oscar Wilde)

film

TOM JONES

autobiography

A BETTER CLASS OF PERSON

A Patriot for Me

AND

A Sense of Detachment

JOHN OSBORNE

FABER AND FABER
London & Boston

A Patriot for Me *was first published in 1966*
and first published as a Faber Paper Covered Edition in 1971
A Sense of Detachment *was first published, in cased and paperback*
editions, in 1973
This edition first published in 1983
by Faber and Faber Limited
3 Queen Square London WC1N 3AU
Typeset in Great Britain by
Goodfellow & Egan Limited Cambridge
Printed in Great Britain by
The Thetford Press Limited Thetford Norfolk
All rights reserved

All applications for professional and amateur rights should be
addressed to Robin Dalton, Robin Dalton Associates,
18 Elm Tree Road, London NW8

Library of Congress Cataloging in Publication
data has been applied for

British Library Cataloguing in Publication Data

Osborne, John, *1929-*
A patriot for me and a sense of detachment.
I. Title
822'.914   PR6029.S39

ISBN 0–571–13041–0

A Patriot for Me

CAST

ALFRED REDL
AUGUST SICZYNSKI
STEINBAUER
LUDWIG MAX VON KUPFER
LT.-COL. LUDWIG VON MÖHL
ADJUTANT
MAXIMILIAN VON TAUSSIG
ALBRECHT
ANNA
HILDE
STANITSIN
COL. MISCHA OBLENSKY
GEN. CONRAD VON HÖTZENDORF
COUNTESS SOPHIA DELYANOFF
JUDGE ADVOCATE JAROSLAV KUNZ
YOUNG MAN IN CAFÉ
PAUL
BARON VON EPP
FERDY
FIGARO
LT. STEFAN KOVACS
MARIE-ANTOINETTE
TSARINA
LADY GODIVA
DR SCHOEPFER
2ND LT. VICTOR JERZABEK
ORDERLY
MISCHA LIPSCHUTZ
MITZI HEIGEL
MINISTER

KUPFER'S SECONDS, PRIVATES,
WAITERS AT ANNA'S, OFFICERS,
WHORES, FLUNKEYS, HOFBURG GUESTS,
CAFÉ WAITERS, GROUP AT TABLE,
BALL GUESTS, SHEPHERDESSES,
BOY, HOTEL WAITERS

The first performance of *A Patriot for Me* was given at the Royal Court Theatre, Sloane Square, London, on 30th June 1965, by the English Stage Society, by arrangement with the English Stage Company. It was directed by Anthony Page and the décor was by Jocelyn Herbert. The musical adviser was John Addison.

The cast was as follows:

ALFRED REDL   Maximilian Schell
AUGUST SICZYNSKI   John Castle
STEINBAUER   Rio Fanning
LUDWIG MAX VON KUPFER   Frederick Jaeger
KUPFER'S SECONDS   Lew Luton, Richard Morgan
PRIVATES   Tim Pearce, David Schurmann, Thick Wilson
LT.-COL. LUDWIG VON MÖHL   Clive Morton
ADJUTANT   Timothy Carlton
MAXIMILIAN VON TAUSSIG   Edward Fox
ALBRECHT   Sandor Eles
WAITERS AT ANNA'S   Peter John, Domy Reiter
OFFICERS   Timothy Carlton, Lew Luton, Hal Hamilton,
          Richard Morgan
WHORES   Dona Martyn, Virginia Wetherell,
          Jackie Daryl, Sandra Hampton
ANNA   Laurel Mather
HILDE   Jennifer Jayne
STANITSIN   Desmond Perry
COL. MISCHA OBLENSKY   George Murcell
GEN. CONRAD VON HÖTZENDORF   Sebastian Shaw
COUNTESS SOPHIA DELYANOFF   Jill Bennett
JUDGE ADVOCATE JAROSLAV KUNZ   Ferdy Mayne
FLUNKEYS   John Forbes, Richard Morgan, Peter John,
          Timothy Carlton

HOFBURG GUESTS Cyril Wheeler, Douglas Sheldon,
          Bryn Bartlett, Dona Martyn, Virginia Wetherell,
          Jackie Daryl, Sandra Hampton, Laurel Mather
CAFÉ WAITERS Anthony Roye, Domy Reiter, Bryn Bartlett,
          Cyril Wheeler
GROUP AT TABLE Dona Martyn, Laurel Mather, Bryn Bartlett,
          Cyril Wheeler
YOUNG MAN IN CAFÉ Paul Robert
PAUL Douglas Sheldon
PRIVATES Richard Morgan, David Schurmann,
          Tim Pearce, Thick Wilson
BARON VON EPP George Devine
FERDY John Forbes
FIGARO Thick Wilson
LT. STEFAN KOVACS Hal Hamilton
MARIE-ANTOINETTE Lew Luton
TSARINA Domy Reiter
LADY GODIVA Peter John
BALL GUESTS Cyril Wheeler, Richard Morgan, Timothy Carlton,
          John Castle, Edward Fox, Paul Robert,
          Douglas Sheldon, Tim Pearce
FLUNKEY David Schurmann
SHEPHERDESSES Franco Derosa, Robert Kidd
DR. SCHOEPFER Vernon Dobtcheff
BOY Franco Derosa
2ND. LT. VICTOR JERZABEK Tim Pearce
HOTEL WAITERS Bryn Bartlett, Lew Luton
ORDERLY Richard Morgan
MISCHA LIPSCHUTZ David Schurmann
MITZI HEIGEL Virginia Wetherell
MINISTER Anthony Roye
VOICES OF DEPUTIES Clive Morton, Sebastian Shaw,
          George Devine, Vernon Dobtcheff,
          Cyril Wheeler
MUSICAL DIRECTOR Tibor Kunstler
MUSICIANS Reg Richman (Bass), Michael Zborowski (Piano),
          Ray Webb (Guitar)

Act One

SCENE 1

A Gymnasium. Of the 7th Galician Infantry Regiment at Lemburg, Galicia, 1890. It appears to be empty. From the high windows on one side, the earliest morning light shows up the climbing bars that run from floor to ceiling. From this, a long, thick rope hangs. Silhouetted is a vaulting horse. The lonely, slow tread of one man's boots is heard presently on the harsh floor. A figure appears. At this stage, his features can barely be made out. It is ALFRED REDL, *at this time Lieutenant. He has close cropped hair, a taut, compact body, a moustache. In most scenes he smokes long black cheroots, like Toscanas. On this occasion, he takes out a shabby cigarette case, an elegant amber holder, inserts a cigarette and lights it thoughtfully. He looks up at the window, takes out his watch and waits. It is obvious he imagines himself alone. He settles down in the half light. A shadow crosses his vision.*

REDL: Who's there? (*Pause.*) Who is it? Come on! Hey!

VOICE: Redl?

REDL: Who is it?

VOICE: Yes. I see you now.

REDL: Siczynski? Is it? Siczynski?

VOICE: Thought it was you. Yes.

> (*A figure appears,* PAUL SICZYNSKI. *He is a strong, very handsome young man about the same age as* REDL, *but much more boyish looking.* REDL *already has the stamp of an older man.*)

SICZYNSKI: Sorry.

REDL: Not at all.

SICZYNSKI: I startled you.

REDL: Well: we're both early.

SICZYNSKI: Yes.

REDL: Still. Not all that much. Cigarette?

(SICZYNSKI *takes one.* REDL *lights it for him.*)

Almost light. I couldn't sleep anyway. Could you?

SICZYNSKI: (*smiles*). I haven't the style for that. Von Kupfer has though. Expect he's snoozing away now. (*Looks at his watch.*) Being wakened by his servant.

Um?

REDL: He gave a champagne supper at Anna's.

SICZYNSKI: Who was invited?

REDL: Half the garrison, I imagine.

SICZYNSKI: Did you go?

REDL: I'm your second . . .

SICZYNSKI: Is that what prevented you being asked?

REDL: It would have stopped me going.

SICZYNSKI: Well then, he'll have stayed there till the last moment, I should think. Perhaps he'll have been worn down to nothing by one of those strapping Turkish whores.

REDL: I doubt it.

SICZYNSKI: His spine cracked in between those thighs. Snapped. . . . All the way up. No, you're most likely right. *You're* right.

REDL: He's popular: I suppose.

SICZYNSKI: Yes. Unlikeable too.

REDL: Yes. He's a good, what's he, he's a good officer.

SICZYNSKI: He's a gentleman. And adjutant, adjutant mark you, of a field battery at the ripe old age of twenty-one. He's not half the soldier you are.

REDL: Well . . .

SICZYNSKI: And now he's on his way to the War College.

REDL: (*quick interest.*) Oh?

SICZYNSKI: Of course. If you'd been in his boots, you'd have been in there and out again by this time, you'd be a major at least, by now (*Pause.*) Sorry—didn't mean to rub it in.

REDL: Kupfer. Ludwig Max Von Kupfer . . . it's cold.

SICZYNSKI: Cigarette smoke's warm.

(*Pause.*)

REDL: How are you?

SICZYNSKI: Cold.

REDL: Here.

SICZYNSKI: Cognac? Your health. Here's to the War College. And you.

REDL: Thank you.

SICZYNSKI: Oh, you will. Get in, I mean. *You* just have to pack in all the effort, while the Kupfers make none at all. He'll be sobering up by now. Putting his aristocratic head under the cold tap and shouting in that authentic Viennese drawl at whoever's picking up after him. You'd better, make it, I mean. Or you'll spend the rest of it in some defeated frontier town with debts. And more debts to look forward to as you go on. Probably the gout.

(*Pause.*) I just hope there isn't ever a war.

(*They smoke in silence. Slightly shy, tense.*

SICZYNSKI *leans against the vaulting horse.*)

REDL: You may underestimate Kupfer.

SICZYNSKI: Maybe. But then he overestimates himself. *You*'ve tremendous resources, reserves, energy. You won't let any old waters close over your head without a struggle first.

REDL: What about you?

SICZYNSKI: (*smiles*). I'm easily disheartened.

REDL: He's destructive, *very* destructive.

SICZYNSKI: Who?

REDL: Kupfer.

SICZYNSKI: Yes, yes. And wilful. Coldly, not too cold, not disinterested.

REDL: That's why I think you underestimate him.

SICZYNSKI: But more vicious than most. You're right there. He's a killer all right.

REDL: Someone'll chalk him up . . . sometime.

SICZYNSKI: What about me?

REDL: That would be very good. Very good.

SICZYNSKI: Just not very likely . . .

REDL: Have you done this before?

SICZYNSKI: (*smiles*). No, never. Have you?

REDL: Only as a bystander.

SICZYNSKI: Well, this time you're a participant. . . . I'd always expected to *be* challenged a hundred times. I never thought

15

I'd do it. Well, picked the right man. Only the wrong
swordsman. May I?
(*He indicates Cognac.* REDL *nods.*)
Have you seen him?

REDL: Seen? Oh, with a sabre. No. Have you?

SICZYNSKI: No. Have you seen *me*?

REDL: Often.

SICZYNSKI: Well, there it is.

REDL: (*softly*). More times than I can think of.

SICZYNSKI: They say only truly illiterate minds are obdurate.
Well, that's me and Kupfer.

REDL: Why do you feel like this about him? He's not exactly
untypical.

SICZYNSKI: Not by any means. For me, well, perhaps he just
plays the part better. He makes me want to be sick. Over
him preferably.

REDL: I don't understand you. You're more than a match for
his sort

SICZYNSKI: I just chose the wrong ground to prove it, here.
(*Pause.*)

REDL: Look, Siczynski, why don't I, I'm quite plausible and
not half a bad actor, for one . . . reason and another, why
don't you let me, sort of . . .

SICZYNSKI: Thank you, Redl. You can't do anything now.

REDL: Very well.

SICZYNSKI: Don't be offended.

REDL: Why should I?

SICZYNSKI: (*wry*). Someone who looks as good as me ought to
be able to handle himself a bit better, don't you agree?

REDL: Yes.

SICZYNSKI: At least—physically. . . . A *little* better don't you
think? Why did you agree to be my second?

REDL: Why did you ask me?

SICZYNSKI: I thought you'd agree to. Did you get anyone else?

REDL: Steinbauer.

SICZYNSKI: As a favour to you? No, I didn't think you'd have
to be persuaded.

REDL: No.

SICZYNSKI: Mine's gone out.
(REDL *offers him a cigarette, from which he takes a light.*)
I thought you always smoked those long Italian cigars.
(REDL *nods.*)
Expensive taste. What is it?
REDL: I was only going to ask-you: *are* you a Jew?
SICZYNSKI: (*smiles*). Grandmother. Maternal Grandmother.
Quite enough though, don't you think? Oh, she became
Catholic when she married my Grandfather. Not that she
ever took it seriously, any more than him. She'd a good
sense of fun, not like the rest of my family. You think it
doesn't matter about Kupfer's insult, don't you? Well of
course you're right. I don't think it would have mattered
what he said. Oh, I quite enjoyed his jokes about calling
me Rothschild. What *I* objected to, from him,—in the
circumstances, was being called Fräulein Rothschild. . . .
REDL: You shouldn't gamble.
SICZYNSKI: I don't.
REDL: On people's goodwill.
SICZYNSKI: I don't. *You* do.
REDL: I do? No, I don't . . . I try not to.
(*He is confused for a moment.* SICZYNSKI *watches him
thoughtfully, through his cigarette smoke. It is getting lighter,
colder.*)
SICZYNSKI: You smell of peppermints.
REDL: Nearly time (*He stands.*)
SICZYNSKI: Kupfer's breath stinks.
REDL: I hadn't noticed.
SICZYNSKI: You mean you haven't got near enough? You don't
need to. *He* should chew peppermints.
(*Pause.*)
Have some of your brandy.
REDL: Thanks.
SICZYNSKI: It's a cold time to be up, to be up at all.
REDL: I've hardly ever had warm feet. Not since I went to
Cadet School.
SICZYNSKI: You work too hard.
REDL: What else can I do?

SICZYNSKI: Sorry. Of course, you're right. I'm just waiting.
Can't think much any more.
(REDL *would like to help if there were some means. But he can't.*)
Go on. If you can, I mean. Don't if you can't . . .
Won't be long, now . . .
REDL: We've never talked together much, have we?
We must have both been here? What? Two years?
SICZYNSKI: Why couldn't you sleep?
REDL: Don't know. Oh yes, I had a dream . . .
SICZYNSKI: But then you're not what they call sociable, are you?
REDL: Aren't I?
SICZYNSKI: Well! Asking for extra duties, poring over all those
manuals.
REDL: You don't make it sound very likeable.
SICZYNSKI: It isn't—much.
(REDL *takes out his watch.*)
REDL: I told Steinbauer two minutes before. He's pretty reliable.
SICZYNSKI: Anyway, you're taking a risk doing *this*. But I suppose
Kupfer will draw the fire.
REDL: And you. You specially.
SICZYNSKI: The Galician Jew, you mean? Yes. But that's only if I
win.
REDL: It needn't come to that.
SICZYNSKI: It will.
REDL: I'll see it doesn't.
SICZYNSKI: No, you won't. You can't. . . What, what does one,
do you suppose, well, look for in anyone, anyone else, I mean?
REDL: For?
SICZYNSKI: Elsewhere.
REDL: I haven't tried. Or thought about it. At least . . .
SICZYNSKI: I mean: That isn't clearly, really, clearly, already in
oneself?
REDL: Nothing, I expect.
(*Pause.*)
SICZYNSKI: Tell me about your dream.
REDL: Do you believe in dreams?
SICZYNSKI: Not specially. They're true while they last, I suppose.
REDL: Well, it wasn't—

18

(*There is the sound of boots. Walking swiftly, confidently, this time. The two men look at each other.*)

Steinbauer. On the dot.

(STEINBAUER *enters.*)

Morning, Steinbauer.

(STEINBAUER *nods, slightly embarrassed. Clicks his heels at* SICZYNSKI.)

Cold.

STEINBAUER: Yes.

SICZYNSKI: Got the cutlery? Oh, yes I see.

STEINBAUER: All here.

SICZYNSKI: Redl was telling me his dream. Go on.

REDL: It's nothing.

SICZYNSKI: That hardly matters, does it?

REDL: Not really time.

SICZYNSKI: Please.

(STEINBAUER *takes out his watch.*)

REDL: Just, oh, I was, well later, I was, I won't tell you the first—

SICZYNSKI: Why not?

REDL: It's too dull. So is *this* too. Anyway: I was attending a court martial. Not mine. Someone else's. I don't quite know whose. But a friend of some sort, someone I liked. Someone upright, frank, respected, but upright. It was quite clear from the start what the outcome would be, and I was immediately worrying about having to go and visit him in gaol. And it wasn't just because I knew I would be arrested myself as soon as I got in there. It wasn't for that. Anyhow, there I was, and I went and started to talk to him. He didn't say anything. There was just the wire netting between us . . . and then of course, they arrested *me*. I couldn't tell whether he was pleased or not. Pleased that I'd come to see him or that they'd got me too. They touched me on the shoulder and told me to stand up, which I did. And by that time he'd gone. Somehow.

(*Sound of several pairs of boots clattering on the unyielding floor into the Gymnasium.* REDL *frowns anxiously at* SICZYNSKI, *who smiles at him. As soon as* KUPFER *and his seconds arrive, they get to their feet. Both sides salute each other and prepare for the duel*

in silence. Sabres are selected. Tunics discarded, etc. All brisk.
The duel begins. The four men watch almost indifferently at first.
But the spectacle soon strips away this. Blood is drawn, sweat
runs, breathing tightens. At one point REDL *steps forward.*
KUPFER *orders him back curtly. All settle down for the end. It*
comes fairly soon.
SICZYNSKI *cries out and falls to the ground.* KUPFER *begins*
dressing almost immediately. He goes out with his companions,
who are trying to be composed.)

STEINBAUER: Shall I? Yes, I'd better get the doctor.

REDL: Yes, I suppose so.

(STEINBAUER *follows the others out.* REDL *wipes the blood from*
SICZYNSKI'*s mouth, cradling him in his arms. He is clearly dead.*)

FADE

SCENE 2

Office of the Commandant, Seventh Galician Infantry Regiment. The
Commandant, LIEUTENANT-COLONEL VON MÖHL, *is seated at his*
desk. A sharp rap at the door. VON MÖHL *grunts. The door is opened*
smartly by the ADJUTANT.

ADJUTANT: Lieutenant Redl, sir.

(REDL *enters, salutes, etc.*)

MÖHL: Is Taussig there?

ADJUTANT: Yes, sir.

MÖHL: Good. All right.

(ADJUTANT *goes out.*)

Redl, Redl, Redl: yes. (*He looks up.*) Sit down, please.

(REDL *sits.* M.OHL *scrutinises him.*)

Well, Redl. You've quite a good deal of news to come it
seems to me. Yes.

REDL: Yes, sir?

MÖHL: You may think that a young officer gets lost among all
the others, that he isn't observed, constantly, critically and
sympathetically. You might think that an officer with an

unremarkable background, or without rather dazzling connections of one sort or another would go unnoticed. Do you think that, Redl?

REDL: Sir, my own experience is that genuine merit rarely goes unnoticed or unrewarded. Even, particularly in the Army.

MÖHL: Good. And quite correct, Redl, and for a very obvious reason. The future of the Empire depends on the Army, probably the future of Europe, on an alert, swift machine that can meet instant crisis from whatever quarter it may come. It's taken us a long time to learn our lesson, lessons like Solferino. Expensive, humiliating and inglorious, but worth it now. Only the very best kind of men can be entrusted in the modern army.

(*He waves at the map of pre-1914 Europe, with Austria-Hungary in the middle, behind him.*)

No one's going to be passed over, every man'll have his chance to prove himself, show what he could do, given half the chance. I don't say there still aren't short cuts for people who don't apparently deserve it, but that's not for you or me to argue. What we *can* do is make sure the way's made to virgin merit, someone with nothing else. What do you say?

REDL: I'm sure you're right, sir.

MÖHL: Oh?

REDL: It always seems quite clear to me, sir, the officers who complain about privilege are invariably inferior or mediocre.

(REDL *speaks coolly and carefully. He is anxious to be courteous and respectful without seeming unctuous, or sound a false, fawning note. He succeeds.*)

MÖHL: Exactly. The real good 'uns don't ever really get left out, that's why so much nonsense is talked, especially about the Army. You can't *afford* to ignore a good man. He's too valuable. A good soldier always knows another one. That's what comradeship is. It's not an empty thing, not an empty thing at all. It's knowing the *value* of other men. And cherishing it. Now: Redl. Two reasons I sent for you. I'll, yes, we'll, I think we'll deal with the best first.

21

(*He pauses.* REDL *waits.*)

As you know, as Commander, it's my duty to recommend
officers for War College examination. This year I only felt
able to recommend Von Taussig, Von Kupfer, and
yourself. The result I can now tell you, after the final
examination and interview, is that you have all three been
granted admission, a very fine achievement for us all. Four
hundred and eighteen candidates for thirty-nine places.
Well, Von Taussig has been admitted number twenty-
eight, yourself twenty-six and Von Kupfer seventeen.
Congratulations.

REDL: Thank you, sir.

MÖHL: Well, I'm very pleased indeed myself, with the result.
All three accepted. It's quite something for me too, you
know, especially over you. I was pretty sure about the
other two, well, of course. . . . But you, well, I knew you
had the education, enough . . . There it is. Now you've
done it.

REDL: I'm very grateful, sir.

MÖHL: By yourself. You. Number twenty-six! Please. Smoke,
if you wish. Here—one of these.
(*Offers him a cigar. Takes one himself.* REDL *lights both of them.*)
So: How do you feel?

REDL: Very proud—and grateful, sir.

MÖHL: I don't think you realize, you've made quite an
impression. Here, listen to this. Arithmetic, algebra,
geometry, trigonometry—all excellent. Elementary
engineering, construction, fortification, geography and
international law, all eighty-five per cent, all first class.
Riding—required standard. That's the only begrudging
remark on any of your reports, required standard. Anyway,
get that horse out in the school a bit. Yes?

REDL: Yes, sir.

MÖHL: Let's see now, what does it say, do you speak Russian?

REDL: No, sir.

MÖHL: No matter. You will. Native language?

REDL: Ruthenian.

MÖHL: German—excellent. Polish, French—fair. Punctilious

22

knowledge military and international matters. Seems to know Franco-Prussian campaign better than anyone who actually took part. Learned. All the qualities of first-class field officer and an unmistakable flair for intelligence. No. Wait a minute, there's more yet. Upright, discreet, frank and open, painstaking, marked ability to anticipate, as well as initiate instructions, without being reckless, keen judgement, cool under pressure—*that*'s Erdmannsdorfer, so that's good, very good indeed—Yes, cool, fine interpreter of the finest modern military thinking. Personality: friendly but unassertive, dignified and strikes everyone as the type of a gentleman and distinguished officer of the Royal and Imperial Army. Well, what do you say?

REDL: I'm overwhelmed, sir.

MÖHL: Well, I like to see this sort of thing happen. Kupfer and Taussig are one thing, and I'm proud of them. But you're another. . . . Yours is effort, effort, concerted, sustained, intelligent effort. Which: brings me to the Siczynski affair. Of course, you realize that if your part in that incident had been made properly known, it would almost certainly have prejudiced your application?

REDL: Yes, sir.

MÖHL: However, we chose to be discreet.

REDL: I'm more grateful than I can tell you, sir.

MÖHL: Well, of course, with Kupfer, it was more difficult. However, he has been in trouble of this kind before, and, let's be honest about it, he does have advantages. He is able to get away with incidents like Siczynski occasionally, though even he can't do it too often. Of course, he was a principal in this case and you weren't, but I must tell you it was a grave error on your part ever to have consented to become involved in an affair which ends in a brother officer's death. I'm saying this to you as a warning for the future. *Don't* get involved.

REDL: Yes, sir. May I ask where is Lieutenant Von Kupfer, sir?

MÖHL: Temporarily transferred to Wiener Neustadt. . . . Was Siczynski a friend of yours?

REDL: No, sir.

MÖHL: What was your opinion of him?

REDL: I hardly knew him, sir. (*Realizes quickly he needs to provide more than this.*) He struck me as being hyper-critical, over-sceptical about things.

MÖHL: What things?

REDL: Army life and traditions, esprit——

MÖHL: Religion?

REDL: We never discussed it. But—yes, I suspect so, I should think . . .

MÖHL: Jewish . . .?

REDL: Yes, sir. I believe.

MÖHL: Galician, like yourself.

REDL: Yes.

MÖHL: You're yes, Catholic, of course.

REDL: Yes, sir.

MÖHL: What about women?

REDL: Siczynski?

(*Nod from* M.OHL.)

As I say, I didn't know him well.

MÖHL: But?

REDL: I never thought of him, no one seemed to, as a ladies' man.

MÖHL: Precisely. Yet he was very attractive, physically, wouldn't you say?

REDL: That's a hard question for another man to answer——

MÖHL: Oh, come, Redl, you know what women are attracted—

REDL: Yes. Of course, I should say he was, quite certainly.

MÖHL: But you never heard of any particular girl or girls?

REDL: No. But then, we weren't exactly, and I don't——

MÖHL: You are a popular officer—Redl—Siczynski wasn't. He had debts, too. And quite hefty ones. Oh, one expects all young officers to have debts. It's always been so, and always will, till they pay soldiers properly. Every other week, a fund has to be raised for this one or that. Fine. But this officer had, or so it seems, and frankly it doesn't surprise me, no friends, was in the hands of moneylenders, of his own race, naturally, and why? Women? Of course, one asks. But who? No one knows. No family. Who was worth nine thousand kroner in debts.

REDL: Nine . . .

MÖHL: Do you think I can find out? It *is* odd, after all. Young
    officer, apparently attractive in many ways, work excellent,
    intelligence exceptional, diligent, manly disposition and all
    the rest of it. Then: where are you?

REDL: Perhaps?—I don't think he was ever in his right element.

MÖHL: Well. There it is. Incident closed now, including your
    part in it.

REDL: Thank you, sir.

MÖHL: Only remember. Involvement. Debts—well, you'll be all
    right. Also, you have friends, and *will* have. As for women, I
    think you know what you're doing.

REDL: I hope so, sir.

MÖHL: What about marriage?

REDL: I'm not contemplating it, not for quite some time, that is.

MÖHL: Good. You've got ideals and courage and fortitude, and
    I'm proud and delighted you'll be going from this regiment
    to War College. You're on your way, Redl. Taussig!
    (ADJUTANT *enters*.)
    Send in Taussig.
    (ADJUTANT *clicks heels. Enter* TAUSSIG *presently*.)
    Ah, Taussig. Come in. You know Redl. You two should have
    something to celebrate together tonight.

FADE

SCENE 3

ANNA's. *A private cubicle. In the background a gipsy orchestra, and flash
young officers eating, drinking, swearing, singing, entertaining* ANNA's
young ladies. REDL *is alone in the cubicle. He leans forward, scoops a
champagne bottle from its bucket to pour himself another glass. It is
empty. He draws the curtain aside and bawls into the smoke and noise.*

REDL: Anna! Anna! Hey! You! What's your name?!
    Max! Leo! Anna! Damn!

(*He gives up. Looks in his tunic for his cigar case. Takes one out, a long black Italian cheroot.* A YOUNG WAITER *enters.*)
Ah, there you are. Thank God. Another—please.
Oh—you've got it. That's clever.

WAITER: I guessed you'd be wanting another, sir.

REDL: Good fellow. Open it, would you?

WAITER: At once, sir.

REDL: Which one are you then?

WAITER: Which one, sir?

REDL: You're not Leo or that other stumpy creature, what's his name—

WAITER: I am Albrecht, sir.

REDL: You're new then.

WAITER: Seven months, sir.

REDL: Oh. I didn't notice you.

WAITER: You don't often do us the honour, sir.

REDL: Light this for me.
(WAITER *does so.*)
I can't afford time for this sort of caper very often.

WAITER: What a magnificent cigar case, sir.

REDL: What? Oh. Yes. Present. From my uncle.

WAITER: Very fine indeed. Shall I pour it now?

REDL: Yes.

WAITER: Pol Roger eighty one, sir.

REDL: (*shortly*). Fine.

WAITER: Would that be crocodile, sir?

REDL: Eh? Oh. Yes. Have you seen my guest anywhere among that mob?

WAITER: Lieutenant Taussig, sir?

REDL: Well, who else?

WAITER: He is talking with Madame Anna.
(REDL *sips his champagne. The* WAITER *has increased his restless, uneasy mood. He can't bring himself to dismiss him yet.*)

REDL: Rowdy, roaring mob you've got in there.

WAITER: Yes, sir.

REDL: Why do they have to make such a damned show?
Howling and vomiting or whoring.

(*They listen.*)

REDL: Drunk. . . . Why do they need to get so drunk?

WAITER: End of the summer manoeuvres they tell me, sir. Always the same then.

REDL: This place'll get put out of bounds one day. Someone should warn Anna.

WAITER: I think she just does her best to please the young officers, sir. Giving them what they ask for.

REDL: They'll get it too, and no mistake. What's that young officer's name?

WAITER: Which one, sir? Oh, with the red-haired girl, Hilde— yes, Lieutenant Steinbauer, sir.

REDL: So it is.

WAITER: Very beautiful girl, sir.

REDL: Yes.

WAITER: Very popular, that one.

REDL: Garbage often is.

WAITER: That's true too, of course, sir.

(*Pause.*)

REDL: Taussig! Where the hell is he?

WAITER: Shall I tell him you want him, sir?

REDL: No. Better not. I'm getting bored sitting here on my own.

WAITER: Can I do anything else, sir?

REDL: No. (*Detaining him.*) Do you remember Kupfer?

WAITER: Lieutenant Kupfer? Oh yes, he used to be in here nearly every night, sometimes when he shouldn't have been. We were sorry when he was re-posted.

REDL: And Lieutenant Siczynski? Do you remember him?

WAITER: No, sir, I don't.

REDL: You don't come from Lemberg?

WAITER: No, sir. From Vienna. Oh, you mean the one who was killed in the duel? He used to come in sometimes, usually on his own. But no one seemed to take much notice of him. He didn't exactly avail himself of the place. Like Lieutenant Kupfer. *He* used to have this cubicle regularly.

REDL: You must miss Vienna.

WAITER: I do, sir. There are always so many different things to

do *there*. In Lemberg everybody knows who you are and
everything about you. . . . Well, no doubt you'll be in
Vienna yourself before long. May I congratulate you, sir?
REDL: Thank you.
WAITER: On the General Staff, I've no doubt, sir.
REDL: We'll see.

(*A roar and banging of tables.*)

What the devil's going on?
WAITER: Lieutenant Steinbauer has passed out, sir.
They're passing him over their heads . . . One by
one . . . Now he's being sick. I'd better go.
REDL: Well, he's better off: see someone takes him home, if
you can.
WAITER: I'll do my best, sir. So, as I say, you'll soon be seeing
for yourself.
REDL: What?
WAITER: Why, Vienna.
REDL: Oh. All I'll see is work. Maps, tactical field work, riding
drill, Russian language, maps.
WAITER: Oh, of course.
REDL: That'll be enough for me.
WAITER: Yes, sir.

(*Pause. Enter* TAUSSIG.)

TAUSSIG: Well, I've fixed us up.
REDL: What?
TAUSSIG: Girls. One each. I've been arguing ten minutes with
Anna, and she insisted she'd only got one spare, that lovely
great black gipsy with the mole on her cheek. There.
WAITER: Zoe.
TAUSSIG: That's the one. So I said to her, I know she's a big
girl, but I know my friend Lieutenant Redl won't go much
on sharing, especially on an occasion like this evening.
REDL: Please forget it. I'm bored with the place.
TAUSSIG: So am I. We'll take another, oh, you've got another,
we'll take some more champagne upstairs with us and be
entertained properly, me by big black Zoe, and you, you
my friend by Hilde. And very lucky you are, doubly lucky,
because she was tied up by young Steinbauer until a few

moments ago, but he's now safely on his face in the cellar, he won't be capable of fulfilling his little engagement tonight, he'll be lucky to stand up on parade in the morning, and Hilde, red, pale, vacant and booked this moment by me is all yours.

REDL: It doesn't matter.

TAUSSIG: Of course, it doesn't. It's all fixed. Fixed by me and paid for.

REDL: Taussig, I can't allow it.

TAUSSIG: Nonsense. It's done.

(WAITER *pours champagne.* TAUSSIG *drinks.*)

You insisted on buying the dinner and champagne. And now, *more* champagne. Now, *I* insist on treating you. Your health.

(*He glances quickly at the* WAITER.)

To black Zoe and her gipsy mole. And Hilde and her red whatever special she's got in there. Drink up.

(REDL *drinks.*)

(*to* WAITER): What are *you* standing about for?

REDL: He was opening the champagne.

TAUSSIG: Well, take another one up. On *my* bill.

REDL: Are you sure?

TAUSSIG: Of course I'm sure. We're going to need it. Come on, I'm glad to see you smoking a cigar again. Can't stand the smell of those peppermints. I've always wanted to tell you. I say, that's a pretty classy case.

REDL: My uncle.

TAUSSIG: I didn't know you had rich relatives.

REDL: Only him.

TAUSSIG: Perhaps I should have let you pay for Hilde yourself.

REDL: Of course. Please.

TAUSSIG: Unless you *would* have preferred Zoe. Sharing, I mean.

REDL: Hilde sounds just the thing.

TAUSSIG: I think she's more your type. Bit on the skinny side. No bottom, little tiny bottom, not a real roly-poly. And breasts made like our friend here. Go on, go and get that other bottle!

29

REDL: (*to* WAITER). Just a moment.

TAUSSIG: I'll round them up.

(*Pause*)

Don't be all night then.

REDL: Just coming.

(*He goes to his wallet, trying not to be awkward. He hands a note to the* WAITER).

WAITER: Thank you, sir.

(*He lights a match for* REDL, *who looks up. Then notices his cigar is out.*)

REDL: Oh, yes.

WAITER: Shall I take this bottle up then, sir?

REDL: Yes. Wait a minute.

(WAITER *pauses.*)

Pour me another glass.

(*He does so. Picks up bucket.*)

WAITER: Good night, sir.

REDL: Good night.

(*The* WAITER *goes out.* REDL *stares into his glass, then drains it, fastens his tunic smartly and steps through the curtain into the tumult.*

FADE

SCENE 4

ANNA'S. *An upstairs room. Bare save for a bed. Lying on it are* HILDE *and* REDL. *Only the outline of their bodies is visible. In the darkness* REDL's *cigar glows. Silence. Then there is an occasional noise from one of the other rooms.*

HILDE: (*whispers*). Hullo. (*Pause.*) Hullo.

REDL: Yes.

HILDE: Alfred! Can't you sleep?

REDL: No. I'm not tired.

HILDE: You slept a little. Oh, not for long. Can I get you anything?

REDL: No thank you.

HILDE: You clench your teeth. Did you know that?

REDL: No.

HILDE: When you're asleep. It makes quite a noise. Scraping together.

REDL: I'm sorry.

HILDE: Oh, please. I didn't mean that. But it'll wear your teeth down. And you've got such nice teeth. You smell of peppermints. Can I put the light on?

REDL: It's your room.

HILDE: It's yours tonight.
(She lights the lamp.)
Some men's mouths are disgusting.

REDL: I'm sure.

HILDE: You look better. You almost fainted. Can't I get you anything? *(Pause.)* Is there any champagne left?
(He pours her some from beside the bed.)
Don't often get champagne bought me. Well, here's to Vienna. Wish I was going.

REDL: Why don't you?

HILDE: I shall, I'm saving up.

REDL: What will you do—the same thing—when you get there?

HILDE: I suppose so. Do you know, your eyes are like mine?

REDL: Are they?

HILDE: I've never seen a man faint before.

REDL: You should be in the army. Do you want to get married?

HILDE: *(softly).* Yes. Of course. Why? Are you proposing?

REDL: I've seen what you've got to offer.

HILDE: Only just. I'm sorry.

REDL: What about?

HILDE: You don't like me.

REDL: What *are* you on about?

HILDE: Never mind. More warm champagne, please.
(He pours.)

REDL: What do you mean? Eh?

HILDE: Nothing. Thank you. God bless. And I hope you'll, you'll be happy in Vienna.

REDL: I'm sorry. Those exams and things have taken it out of me. Perhaps I'll come back tomorrow.

HILDE: Was Lieutenant Siczynski a friend of yours?

REDL: No. Why, did you know him?

HILDE: I used to see him.

REDL: Did he——

HILDE: No. Not with anyone. He usually sat on his own in a corner, reading the foreign papers or just drinking. I used to look at his eyes. But he never looked at me.

(REDL *leans over the bed and kisses her lingeringly. She returns the embrace abstractedly. He looks down at her.*)

Peppermints!

REDL: Damn it! I apologized, didn't I?

(*She puts her finger to his mouth to calm him.*)

HILDE: *And* cigars. That's what you smell of, and horses and saddles. What could be nicer, and more manly?

REDL: You're very, very pretty, Hilde. I love your red hair.

HILDE: You don't have to make love to me, Alfred. I'm only a whore.

REDL: But I mean it.

HILDE: Hired by your friend.

REDL: Pretty little, brittle bones.

HILDE: Lieutenant Taussig.

REDL: Is that him, next door?

HILDE: (*listens*). At this moment, I should say.

(*They listen.*)

Is he a good friend of yours?

REDL: I can't say I'd call anyone I know a good friend.

HILDE: Are you sure you can't sleep?

REDL: Yes . . . But why don't you?

HILDE: May I put my head on your arm?

REDL: If you wish . . .

HILDE: No, I'll finish my champagne. Do you like children?

REDL: Yes. Why?

HILDE: Would you like some of your own?

REDL: Very much. Wouldn't you?

HILDE: Yes, I would.

REDL: Then what's stopping you?

HILDE: One would like to be loved, if it's possible.

REDL: Love's hardly ever possible.

HILDE: Do you believe that?

REDL: Yes. Anyway, there are always too many babies being born. So—

HILDE: You may be right. Perhaps that's why you're in the army.

REDL: What's the matter with you? I'm in the army because it suits *me* and I'm suited to *it*. I can make my own future. I can style it my own way.

HILDE: What about Siczynski?

REDL: He wasn't suited to it. Who's in that other room, there?

HILDE: Albrecht . . . Would you like to go?

REDL: No. I just asked you a question, that's all. Albrecht who?

HILDE: The waiter you were talking to while I was with the young lieutenant.

(*Pause.*)

REDL: He's a noisy fellow.

HILDE: Or whoever's with him.

(*They listen. She watches* REDL's *face.*)

Your cigar's gone out. Here. He always gets the pick, Albrecht. Anything he wants. Anyone.

(*She moves over to the wall and pulls back a flap and looks through.*)

Come here.

REDL: What for?

(*But he joins her.*)

HILDE: Do you want to look?

(*He hesitates, then does so. She returns to the bed, empties the champagne into her glass, and watches him. Presently, he turns away and sits on the bed. She puts her arm round his shoulder. Offers him drink.*)Have some?

(*He shakes his head.*)

Sad?

REDL: No. Not sad. One always just wishes that a congenial evening had been—even more congenial.

HILDE: Think I'll go to bed. It's made me sleepy again.

(REDL *listens.*)

Shall I turn the light out?

(*He nods. She does so. He goes to the window and looks out.*)

33

Presently—)
Good night, Alfred.

REDL: Good night, Hilde.

HILDE: Sorry. I can't keep awake. But you don't mind . . .

(*He looks across at her, puts on his tunic, takes out a bank note, picks up his cap.*)

REDL: Good night, Hilde. Thank you.

(*He presses the note into her hand.*)

HILDE: I'll tell your friend you left in time for reveille.

(*He turns.*)

Alfred——

(*She sits up and kisses him lightly.*)

You have the most beautiful mouth that ever, ever kissed me. Good night, Lieutenant.

REDL: Good night.

HILDE: (*sleepily*). You'll be a colonel one day. On the General Staff. Or even a general.

(*He gazes down at her, re-lights his cigar. The noise from the adjoining room has subsided. He slips out.*)

FADE

SCENE 5

Warsaw. A darkened office. The light from a magic lantern shines white on a blank screen which faces the audience. A figure is seen to be operating it. Another, seated in front of it, is watching the screen. The first figure is LIEUTENANT STANITSIN. *The second* COLONEL OBLENSKY.

OBLENSKY: Next!

STANITSIN: Redl.

(REDL's *photograph in uniform on the screen.*)

Alfred Von Redl. Captain. Seventh Galician Infantry Regiment. Lemberg. Born Lemberg March 4th, 1864. Family background: parents Leopold and Marthe Redl. Eighth of eleven children. Father ex-horse trooper, now second-grade clerical worker Royal and Imperial Railway. Religion: Catholic. Education: Cadet School, passed out with honours. Equitation school.

OBLENSKY: Oh, do get to the meat, Stanitsin. I want my dinner.

STANITSIN: (*flustered slightly*). Oh—just——

OBLENSKY: If there is any. They're not a very promising lot this time, are they?

STANITSIN: Passed out of War College May of last year, number twenty-three of his entry, recommended particularly, on pink paper, recommended.

OBLENSKY: (*turns head*). So it is. Meticulous.

STANITSIN: For appointment on General Staff.

OBLENSKY: Yes.

STANITSIN: Health: periodic asthma while at Cadet School, twice almost leading to his discharge. However, in the past ten years, this complaint seems to have been almost completely overcome. Contracted syphilis two and a half years ago, underwent treatment and discharged Lemberg Military Hospital. One serious breach of discipline, involved in duel when fellow officer was killed. Acted as one of the officer's seconds. Affair hushed up and Redl reprimanded. Otherwise unblemished record sheet. Present duty: shortly returned from nine months on staff of Military Attaché in St. Petersburg, ostensibly learning Russian language.

OBLENSKY: Probably all he did do. That's all *ours* do in Vienna. Pick up German in that atrocious, affected accent. I don't know why either of us bothers to observe—just young officers going to diplomatic functions, learning the language painstakingly, like an English governess, and about as well, and not a secret in sight. Most of them just come back like Redl, with the clap at least, or someone else's crabs. Well?

STANITSIN: Waiting for new posting. Financial affairs: No source of income apart from army pay. Although he seems to have invented a fond uncle who occasionally gives him fancy presents or gratuities, of whom there is no trace. Debts, not exactly serious, are considerable. They include:

tailor, the biggest trade debt, outstanding accounts at various cafés, restaurants, bootmakers, livery, wine merchants and cigar—

OBLENSKY: Oh, come along, friend. What else?

STANITSIN: Not much. Two moneylenders, small, Fink, Miklas also.

OBLENSKY: Oh—Miklas. I know him. How much?

STANITSIN: Together, some twenty-two hundred kronen.

OBLENSKY: Yes?

STANITSIN: He is also negotiating the lease of a thirdfloor apartment in the Eighth District.

OBLENSKY: Yes?

STANITSIN: That's about it.

OBLENSKY: Personal?

STANITSIN: Studious. Popular with fellow officers.

OBLENSKY: Oh, come along: women?

STANITSIN: Occasionally. Nothing sustained.

OBLENSKY: Spare time?

STANITSIN: Work mostly. Otherwise cafés, reading foreign newspapers, drinking with friends.

OBLENSKY: All army?

STANITSIN: Mostly.

OBLENSKY: Languages?

STANITSIN: Ruthenian native. Polish, German, some French.

OBLENSKY: And Russian. Some. Yes?

STANITSIN: I'm sorry?

OBLENSKY: What else? If anything.

STANITSIN: That's all, sir.

OBLENSKY: All right. Clever, brilliant officer, unpromising background. Ambitious. Bit extravagant. Popular. Diligent. What do you want to do?

STANITSIN: Continue surveillance, sir?

OBLENSKY: Unpromising lot. Very well. Get me a drink. Ah— good. Redl. Yes. All right. Background: nil. Prospects of brilliant military career exceptional. What he needs now, at this exact stage, is a good, advantageous marriage. An heiress is the ideal. But a rich widow would do even better. He probably needs someone specially adroit socially, a good

listener, sympathetic, a woman other men are pleased to
call a friend and mean it. Experienced. He knows what he
wants, I dare say. He just needs someone to unobtrusively
provide the right elements . . . Perhaps we should think
about it . . . Anyway, remind me—sometime next week.
Right. Come on then. Next!
STANITSIN: Kupfer.

(REDL's *photograph is switched abruptly from the screen and
replaced by* KUPFER's.)
Kupfer. Ludwig Max Von Kupfer. Major.

FADE

SCENE 6

*A terrace in the Hofburg, the Emperor's residence in Vienna. Through
the french windows, naturally, is where the court ball is going on, with the
aristocracy, diplomatic corps, officers of the Royal and Imperial Army,
flunkeys, etc. Talking to* VON MÖHL *is Chief of the General staff,
General* CONRAD VON HÖTZENDORF.

MÖHL : Haven't been here for years.
HÖTZENDORF: Oh?
MÖHL : It's good to be back.
HÖTZENDORF: I'm sure.
MÖHL : There's nowhere quite like it, really, is there?
HÖTZENDORF: No. There's not.
MÖHL : Not where I've been, anyway. What about you,
    General?
HÖTZENDORF: No, no I don't think so.
MÖHL : I haven't been here since, oh, well, when was it, well I
    was a young captain, and I was in the Railway Bureau.
HÖTZENDORF: Were you?
MÖHL : Wiry. I could bend, do anything. Like a willow.
    Where's your wife, General? Would you like me—
HÖTZENDORF: No. She's all right. She's somewhere . . . Paris,
    that's the nearest to it, I suppose.

MÖHL: Yes.

HÖTZENDORF: But really, altogether different.

MÖHL: Entirely.

HÖTZENDORF: In Vienna, well, everyone is bourgeois, or whatever it is, and a good thing too, everyone, the beggars in the street, kitchen maids, the aristocracy and, let's be honest, the Emperor.

MÖHL: Yes.

HÖTZENDORF: And they all of them enjoy themselves. In Paris, well, in my experience, they're all pretending to be bohemians, from top to bottom, and all the time, every one of them are tradesmen. Well, I don't think you're a real bohemian if you've one eye—or *both* eyes in the case of Paris—on the cash box.

MÖHL: Quite.

HÖTZENDORF: Yes. That's Paris. That's the French. Trouble with Vienna: seems to have old age built into it.

MÖHL: Still that's better than moving on to God knows what, *and* in such an ugly way, like Prussia, for instance.

HÖTZENDORF: Yes. Or England. Even more. They'll soon wreck it. Prussians *are* efficient. English wilful. There *is* a difference. Still, all *we* do is celebrate and congratulate ourselves on saving Europe from the infidel.

MÖHL: I know . . . There's little credit for it.

HÖTZENDORF: Still. It *was* a long time ago.

MÖHL: Redl!

(*He hails* REDL *from the ballroom, who appears.*)

Redl, my dear boy! What a pleasant surprise. General, may I? Captain Alfred Redl: General Von Hötzendorf.

(*They acknowledge.*)

Since I last saw you, Redl, I now have the honour of working on the General's staff.

REDL: Indeed, sir. Congratulations.

MÖHL: Redl was just about the finest young officer, all round, when I was commandant in Lemberg, for eleven years.

HÖTZENDORF: So you told me. Who was the very pretty young lady you were dancing with?

REDL: I'm sorry, sir, which one?

38

MÖHL: Hah! Which *one*!

HÖTZENDORF: Small-boned, dark, brown eyes.

REDL: Miss Ursula Kunz, sir.

HÖTZENDORF: Kunz?

MÖHL: Ah, Kunz. Miss Kunz, youngest daughter of Judge Advocate Jaroslaw Kunz.

HÖTZENDORF: Ah.

MÖHL: Good man. Very.

HÖTZENDORF: Is he?

MÖHL: Seems to be.

HÖTZENDORF: Would you agree, Redl?

REDL: I, sir? From the little I know, and have been able to observe reliably, he is very competent indeed.

HÖTZENDORF: No more?

REDL: Accomplished, too . . . Unpopular.

HÖTZENDORF: Why?

REDL: I don't know, sir.

HÖTZENDORF: I believe it. Something odd, don't know what.

MÖHL: Well—yes . . . But how useful.

HÖTZENDORF: Oh, yes. Useful. Remember what Radetsky said about General Haynau? He said about Haynau, let's see: 'He's my best general all right, but he's like a razor. When you've used him, put him back in his case'.

MÖHL: The General was talking about Vienna, Redl. Well—— How are *you* enjoying it?

REDL: Very much, sir.

MÖHL: Better than St. Petersburg?

REDL: The Russians find it very difficult to enjoy life. Although they *do* manage occasionally.

HÖTZENDORF: Yes. Yes, but, you know, this is a great place to do *nothing*, sit in a café, and dream, listen to the city, *do nothing* and not even anticipate regretting it.

MÖHL: Ah, there's friend Kunz.

HÖTZENDORF: Who? Where?

MÖHL: With the Countess Delyanoff.

HÖTZENDORF: So he is.

MÖHL: You know her?

HÖTZENDORF: Just.

MÖHL: I think they're coming out here.

HÖTZENDORF: (*to* REDL). . . . . Sort of woman, know her——?
(REDL *shakes his head.*)
Well, the sort of woman who looks at you for five minutes without a word and then says 'what do you think about Shakespeare?' Or, something like that. Unbelievable.

MÖHL: Ah, Kunz! Countess.
(*Enter* MAJOR JAROSLAW KUNZ *and the* COUNTESS SOPHIA DELYANOFF.)
We were just watching you.
(MÖHL *makes the introductions, leaving* REDL *till last.*)

COUNTESS: We've met before.

REDL: Forgive me——

COUNTESS: Oh, yes. Not once, but at least three times. You were on General Hauser's staff in St. Petersburg, and a short spell in Prague, were you not?

REDL: I'm sorry.

COUNTESS: Please. I'm sure you had no eye——

MÖHL: Oh, come, Countess, I can't think of anyone more likely to get his eye fixed on someone like you. You're being unfair.

COUNTESS: No. I think not. But I forgive him.
(*A* FLUNKEY *presents glasses of champagne.*)

MÖHL: The General and I were just talking about Vienna.

KUNZ: Yes.

MÖHL: We were just saying—there's nowhere quite like it.

KUNZ: No. You've been away some time, I believe, Colonel. Where was it?

MÖHL: Przemysl.

KUNZ: Przemysl. Ah yes, with all the fortifications.

MÖHL: Four twelve-inch howitzers, some nine- and some six-inch, forty battalions, four squadrons, forty-three artillery companies, eight sapper companies—oh, please forgive me.

KUNZ: Yes. Nowhere quite like Przemysl, in fact.

COUNTESS: I'm afraid I simply can't understand the army, or why any man is ever in it.

HÖTZENDORF: Nor should you. The army's like nothing else. It goes beyond religion. It serves everyone and everyone serves it, even Hungarians and Jews. It conscripts, but it calls the best men out, men who'd never otherwise have been called on.

KUNZ: I think perhaps it's a little like living in the eighteenth century; the army. Apart from Przemysl, that is. Still that *is* a Viennese speciality? Don't you think, General?

HÖTZENDORF: I see nothing about the eighteenth century that makes me believe the nineteenth was any better. And what makes *you* think that the twentieth will be an improvement?

KUNZ: But why do you assume *I* should think it would be?

COUNTESS: I don't think I could ever have been a soldier. I'd want to be a stranger in a street, a key on a concierge's board, inaccessible if I wanted.

MÖHL: But that's what a *soldier* is.

COUNTESS: Only at the cost of his identity. Wouldn't you say, Captain? (*To* REDL.)

REDL: I think the General's right. The army creates an élite.

COUNTESS: No. I believe *it* is created. The army. It can't change. And it is changed from outside.

MÖHL: Nothing else trains a man——

KUNZ: Aptitudes, aptitudes at the expense of character.

COUNTESS: But it can, in its own way, provide a context of expression for people, who wouldn't otherwise have it.

KUNZ: I can only say, Countess, you can have met very few soldiers.

COUNTESS: You're quite wrong, Major. Why, look at me now. Several hundred guests and who am I with? The Chief of the General Staff himself, a distinguished Colonel from Przemysl, a Judge Advocate Major from Vienna and a splendid young Captain. And how different you all are, each one of you. I must say: I can't think of anything more admirable than not having to play a part.

KUNZ: I'm sorry, Countess, but nonsense! We all play parts, *are* doing so now, *will* continue to do so, and as long as we are playing at being Austrian, Viennese, or whatever we think we are, cosmopolitan and nondescript, a position palmed on us by history, by the accident of having held back the Muslim horde at the gates of Europe. For which no one is grateful, after all, it was two centuries ago, and we resent it,

41

feel ill-used and pretend we're something we're not, instead of recognizing that we're the provincial droppings of Europe. The Army, all of *us*, and the Church, sustain the Empire, which is what, a convenience to other nations, an international utility for the use of whoever, Russia, England or Francis Joseph, which again, is what? Crown Imperial of non-intellect. Which is why, for the moment, it survives. Like this evening, the Hofball, perspiring gaiety and pointlessness.

(*Pause.*)

HÖTZENDORF: Countess, please excuse me.

KUNZ: Plus a rather heavy odour of charm.

(HÖTZENDORF *clicks his heels and goes out.*)

COUNTESS: (*to* MÖHL). I'm sorry if I've offended the General.

KUNZ: *I* offended, not you, Countess.

MÖHL: Correct. He's not accustomed to your kind of young banter, Kunz.

KUNZ: I didn't expect him to take me so seriously.

COUNTESS: (*smiles*). Of course you did.

MÖHL: He is still the finest officer in the Royal and Imperial Army.

KUNZ: Very probably.

MÖHL: He is an old friend. He may not be as clever as you, Major, but his heart is in the right place.

KUNZ: Where it can be seen by everyone.

MÖHL: And I will not stand by and allow him to be sneered at and insulted.

KUNZ: I quite agree. Please excuse me, Countess. Gentlemen.

COUNTESS: Well. What tempers you men do have! What about you, Captain, we've not heard much out of you yet? I've a feeling you're full of shocking things.

REDL: What about?

COUNTESS: Why, what we've been talking about.

REDL: Like the army, you mean? I'm afraid I don't agree with the Major.

COUNTESS: No?

REDL: No. I mean, for myself, I didn't want to be, or mean to be: rigid or fixed.

COUNTESS: But you're not.

REDL: No. At the same time, there must be bonds, some bonds that have more meaning than others.

COUNTESS: I don't follow.

MÖHL: Now you're baiting, Countess. Of course he's right. No officer should be allowed to speak in the way of Major Kunz.

COUNTESS: He offends against blood. He——

MÖHL: Against himself; it's like being a Pole or a Slovak or a Jew, I suppose. All these things have more meaning than being, say, a civil servant, or a watchmaker. And all these things are brought together in the army like nowhere else. It's the same experience as friendship or loving a woman, speaking the same tongue, that is a *proper* bond, it's *human*, you can see it and experience it, more than 'all men are brothers' or some such nonsense.

COUNTESS: And do *you* agree with that, Captain Redl?

REDL: I don't agree that all men are brothers, like Colonel Möhl. We are clearly not. Nor should be, or ever want to be.

COUNTESS: Spoken like a true aristocrat.

REDL: Which, as you must know, I am not——

COUNTESS: Oh, but I believe you are. Don't you, Colonel?

REDL: We're meant to clash. And often and violently. I am proud to be despised by some men, no perhaps most men. Others are to be tolerated or ignored. And if they do the same for me, I am gratified, or, at least, relieved.

MÖHL: I agree with the Countess about you, Redl. He has style, always had it, must have had it as a tiny boy.

COUNTESS: Your pride in the Captain is quite fierce, Colonel. It's quite touching.

MÖHL: I don't know about touching, as you call it . . . it's *real*, anyhow.

COUNTESS: But that's only too clear, and why not? It's quite obviously justified.

MÖHL: Some men have a style of living like bad skins. Coarse grained, erupting, spotty. Let me put it this way: I don't have to tell you that, even in this modern age of what they call democracy, the army is still a place of privilege. Redl is the rare type that redeems that privilege. And why? Because he overpowers it, overpowers it by force, not mob-trained force, but natural, disciplined character, ability and honour. And that's all I've got to say on the subject.

COUNTESS: My dear Colonel, I don't know who is the most embarrassed—you or Captain Redl.

REDL: Myself, Countess. A truly honest man is never embarrassed.

COUNTESS: You mean: *you* are not honest?

MÖHL: The boy's an open book. He should be in Intelligence. No one would believe him!

COUNTESS: But not tolerant.

REDL: I don't think so.

COUNTESS: Oh, indeed, I think you ignore what doesn't interest you. Which is why you didn't remember me in spite of the fact of our having met on three separate occasions.

REDL: Pardon me, Countess. I remembered immediately after.

COUNTESS: You think I am a snob because I accused you of trumpeting like an aristocrat just now. *You* are the snob, Captain Redl, not I. As Colonel Von Möhl here will tell you, my husband was a petty landowner from Cracow and *I* am the daughter of a veterinary surgeon.

MÖHL: (*laughs*). Well, don't take that too seriously, Redl.

COUNTESS: Colonel: I appeal to you!

MÖHL: Well, let me say you would say there was only *some* truth in it.

(*He chuckles again. A* FLUNKEY *approaches* REDL *with a salver with a card on it.*)

FLUNKEY: Captain Redl, sir?

REDL: Please excuse me.

(*He takes the card out of the envelope, reads it, hands it to* MÖHL.)

MÖHL: Archduke Ferdinand . . . Ah, well, you'd better get along! Quickly. Here, you!

(*Grabs more champagne glasses from passing* FLUNKEY.)

Get this down you first. Very beautiful, if I may say so. Redl! Countess, your health. The Archduke's the man now. Ferdinand's the one to watch, and I think he's probably all right. Knows what he's doing. Knows what's going on in the

Empire, Hungary, for instance, Serbia. You see, the
Belvedere, that's going to be the centre of things, not the
Hofburg any more. Pity that, about all that, what do you call
it, morganatic marriage business.

COUNTESS: Yes, indeed. Poor woman. Having to trail behind
countesses, a hundred yards behind him.

MÖHL: Why do you think he married her?

COUNTESS: Why does any man get married?

REDL: Children, property.

COUNTESS: But one sees all that, but it couldn't have operated in
this case. He could have had her as his mistress like his
uncle. But then, when you think of the men one knows who
are married, and who they're married *to*, and what their real,
snotty little longings are underneath their proud watch and
chains, their constant broken, sidelong glances. Oh, I know
all about it, even if it's difficult to understand sometimes.
Captain, you mustn't keep His Imperial Highness waiting.
Not while *I* lecture you on marriage.

(REDL *clicks his heels and leaves them.*)

MÖHL: Well!

COUNTESS: Yes, Colonel.

MÖHL: I was just thinking, what you were saying about marriage
then.

COUNTESS: And——?

MÖHL: It really is the most *lamentable* thing for most of us, isn't
it? I mean, as you say, it doesn't work really. Only the
appearances function. Eh? Everyone knows the *feelings*, but
what's the answer, what's the answer do you think?

COUNTESS: The only answer is not to be drawn into it, like the
Captain.

MÖHL: No, I think you're wrong there. Redl would make a first-
class husband.

COUNTESS: You think so?

MÖHL: Absolutely. He's steadfast, sober, industrious, orderly,
he likes orderly things, hates chaos. That's why marriage
would suit him so well. That's what marriage represents, I
suppose. I say, I *am* enjoying talking to you.

COUNTESS: And I am enjoying talking to you. Do you think
  Captain Redl will come back to us?
MÖHL: Oh, I should think so. Order out of chaos. I know, we'll
  keep an eye out for him, learn what the Archduke had to say
  to him. You wouldn't care to dance with such an old man,
  would you?
COUNTESS: But, of course, delighted. Major Kunz is a very
  uninspired dancer.
MÖHL: That's because he doesn't like it. Now *I* love it. I'm so
  glad Redl got that invitation. Good boy! Oh, I say, I *am*
  having a good time.
  (*He beams boyishly, offers his arm to her, and they leave the
  terrace to join the dancers in the ballroom.*)

FADE

SCENE 7

One drawing room of COUNTESS DELYANOFF'*s house. One oil lamp burns
on a desk. On a chair are* REDL'*s tunic, sword, and cap and gloves. A
sharp, clear, moaning cry is heard. Once, quickly. Then again, longer,
more violent. Then silence. Fumbling footsteps outside the door.* REDL
*enters in his breeches, putting on his vest, carrying his boots. He slumps
into a chair, dropping the boots beside him. A voice outside calls softly:
'Alfred, Alfred!'*

  The COUNTESS *enters swiftly, anxious, her hair down to her waist,
very beautiful in her nightgown. She looks across at* REDL *as if this had
happened before, goes to a decanter and pours a brandy. With it, she
crosses to* REDL'*s armchair and looks down at him.*

REDL: Sophia?
COUNTESS: My dear?
REDL: Sorry I woke you.
COUNTESS: I should think you woke the entire street.
REDL: Sorry. So sorry.
COUNTESS: Don't be silly. Here.

(*She hands him the brandy. He takes some. Stares at his boots.*)

REDL: I think I'd better go.

COUNTESS: It's early yet. Why, it's only, I can't see, look, it's only half-past one.

REDL: Still . . .

COUNTESS: You left me *last* night at three. And when you're gone I can't sleep. I wake the moment you've gone. All I can do is think about you.

REDL: I know. Please forgive me . . . Better put these on. (*Takes one of the boots.*)

COUNTESS: Alfred. Please come back to bed . . . I know you hate me asking you, but I do beg you . . . Just for an hour. You *can't* go out now.

REDL: I need some air.

COUNTESS: (*softly*) Darling—

REDL: Need my orderly on these occasions. Can't get my boots on. (*She grasps his knee and kneels.*)

COUNTESS: Why did you wake?

REDL: Oh: Usual.

COUNTESS: And you're crying again.

REDL: I know. . . . (*His face is stony. His voice firm.*) Why do you always have to look at me?

COUNTESS: Because I love you.

REDL: You'd look away . . .

COUNTESS: That's why. What can I do, my darling?

REDL: Nothing . . . I must get these damned things . . . (*Struggles with boots*). I'd love another brandy. (*She rises and gets it.*) It's like a disease.

COUNTESS: What is?

REDL: Oh, all this incessant, *silly* weeping. It only happens, it creeps up on me, when I'm asleep. No one else has ever noticed it . . . Why do you have to wake up?

COUNTESS: Here. Alfred: don't turn away from me.

REDL: My mouth tastes sour.

COUNTESS: I didn't mean that. Anyway, what if it is? Don't turn your head away.

47

(*She grasps his head and kisses him. He submits for a moment, then thrusts her away.*)

REDL: Please!

COUNTESS: What is it? Me?

REDL: No. You're—you're easily the most beautiful . . . desirable woman I've ever . . . There couldn't be . . .

COUNTESS: It's not easy to believe.

REDL: Sophia: it's *me*. It's like a disease.

COUNTESS: You must feel deeply. So do I. Why do you think you've got *me* crying as well. No one's done that to me for years!

REDL: It's like, I can't . . .

COUNTESS: (*impatient*). But it *isn't* like the clap you got off some garrison whore. That's all over. You know it, you were cured, cured, you've got a paper to say so, and even if you weren't do you think I would care?

REDL: It isn't that.

COUNTESS: Then what is it? Why do you dream? Why do you sweat and cry out and *leave* me in the middle of the night? Oh, God!

(*She recovers.*)

REDL: Here, have some of this, I'll get some more.

COUNTESS: No, that's fine.

REDL: Why don't you commit yourself?

COUNTESS: Why don't *you*? My darling, try not to drink so much.

REDL: I've told you. I drink. I drink, heavily sometimes, I don't get *drunk*.

COUNTESS: Yes. So you say.

REDL: It's the truth.

COUNTESS: What are you saying? No, forget I asked. Don't take any of this as *true*, Alfred, I beg of you. It's early in the morning, everything's asleep and indifferent now— *threatening to us*, both of us, *you're* in tears, you wake up in a depression, in a panic, you're dangerous and frightened again and I'm in tears. Please, don't, please, stay, stay with me, I'll look after you, I'll make up . . . at least for something. I'll protect you, protect you . . . and love you.

48

REDL: I can protect myself.

COUNTESS: But you can't. Not *always*. Can you? What is it?

REDL: I must go. I can't sit here.

COUNTESS: Why can't you trust me?

REDL: I've told you . . . I *don't* mean to hurt you.

COUNTESS: And I believe you.

REDL: I just can't.

(*Pause.*)

COUNTESS: Have you never confided in anyone?

REDL: No.

COUNTESS: Hasn't there ever been anyone? (*Pause.*)
What about another man? I know friendship means a lot to
you . . . What about Taussig?

REDL: No. At least . . . Only a very, a very little. I did try
one evening. But he doesn't welcome confidences. He
doesn't know what to do with them . . . or where to put
them.

COUNTESS: You mean nobody else, not *one*, your mother, your
grandfather, no one?

REDL: They might have been;——

COUNTESS: Um?

REDL: But I never did.

COUNTESS: Why?

REDL: I suppose I . . . they, *I* waited too long, and
then . . . they were killed. An accident. You're shivering.

COUNTESS: Please try. Everyone owes something to someone.
You *are* in love with me, Alfred, I know you are, and
you've told me yourself. That must be something.

REDL: Put this on.

(*He places his tunic round her shoulders.*)

COUNTESS: What about you?

(*He shrugs.*)

You look better. *Are* you?

REDL: Yes. At least they go quickly. Just at a bad time. In the
night. Or when I'm having to force myself to do something
as an exercise, or a duty, like working late.

COUNTESS: I tell you: you work too hard.

REDL: Or sometimes I get caught in some relaxation. Sitting in

a café, listening to gossip, and I enjoy that after a long day, and I'm curious. But if I listen to a conversation that's got serious, say, about politics, the Magyars or merging with Germany, or something like that, I feel myself, almost as if I were falling away and disappearing. I want to run.
. . . But, I've felt I should take a serious, applied interest in this sort, in, ours is a complicated age, and I'm some small part of it, and I should devote as much attention and interest to it as I can muster. I should be giving up time—

COUNTESS: What time, for heaven's sake? You already——

REDL: Much more than I do, *much* more. I used not even to try.

COUNTESS: You mean *I* waste it?

REDL: But I can't relax or be at ease.

COUNTESS: Why are you so watchful? You always seem to be at the ready in some way, listening for something . . . some stray chance thing.

REDL: I don't know what that means.

(*He goes to the decanter.*)

COUNTESS: Please, Alfred. You've an early train in the morning . . .

REDL: Do you know: the only time I drink heavily is when I'm with you? No, I didn't mean that. But when you're badgering me and sitting on my head and, and I can't breathe.

COUNTESS: Why do you always have to make love to me with the——

REDL: There you go!

COUNTESS: Why? Why do you insist? Before we even begin?

REDL: I might ask you why *you* insist on turning the light on.

COUNTESS: Because I want to look at your face. Is that so strange?

REDL: You must know, *you* must know, we're not all the same.

COUNTESS: Why do you never kiss me?

REDL: But I do.

COUNTESS: But never in bed.

REDL: Oh, let's go back. We're tired.

COUNTESS: And turn your head away?

50

REDL: Damn your eyes, I *won't* be catechized!

COUNTESS: Why do you never speak?

REDL: What do you want out of me? Well, I tell you, whatever it is, I *can't* give it. Can't and won't.
(*Pause.*)

COUNTESS: I thought it was only whores you didn't kiss or speak to.

REDL: You would know more about that.
(*She looks up at him miserably, shivering. He feels outmanoeuvred. Takes his tunic from her and puts it on.*)
Excuse me.

COUNTESS: If you leave me, you'll be alone.

REDL: That's what I want, to be left alone.

COUNTESS: You'll always be alone.

REDL: Good. Splendid.

COUNTESS: No it isn't. You know it isn't. That's why you're so frightened. You'll fall alone.

REDL: So does everyone. Even if they don't know it.

COUNTESS: You can't be *saved* alone.

REDL: I don't expect to be saved, as you put it. Not by you.

COUNTESS: Or any other woman?

REDL: Or anyone at all.
(*He picks up his cap and gloves.*)

COUNTESS: What have I done?

REDL: *I* am the guilty one. Not you. Please forgive me.

COUNTESS: Don't, don't go. (*Pause.*) One feels very old at this time of night.
(*She goes to the window. He watches her, distressed.*)
It's the time of night when people die. People give up.
(*He goes behind her, hesitates, puts his head against hers for comfort. Pause.*)
You can't have your kind of competitive success *and* seclusion.
(*He sighs, draws away and goes to the door.*)

REDL: Good night, Sophia.

COUNTESS: Good night.
(*Pause.*)

REDL: Would you like to have tea?

COUNTESS: When?
REDL: Tuesday?
COUNTESS: I can't.
REDL: Wednesday?
COUNTESS: Please.
  (*He turns.*)
  Yes, please.
  (*He goes out.*)

FADE

SCENE 8

OBLENSKY's *office. He is reading a letter to* STANITSIN.

OBLENSKY: 'In haste. Enroute for Prague. Wherever I am, my
  dearest, you will trouble my heart. I can say no more, I
  cannot think. The work here will do me good I expect. Try
  to do something yourself. This is a difficult time. I seem
  to: seem to——'can't read it—'speak . . . speak out of
  nowhere. You deserve only the best, not the worst. Forgive
  me: Alfred'. Where's hers? Ah: 'My dearest love, why are
  you writing to me like this? You seem to have forgotten
  everything. It was not all like those short times during the
  night. The rest *was* different'—underlined. 'Don't, I beg
  you, *don't* deceive yourself. Why don't you answer my
  letters? I wait for them. Give me a word, or something that
  will do. At least something I can go over. I can do nothing.
  Now *I* am helpless. Loved one, don't something this.
  Forever, your Sophia. P.S. Did you never intend coming
  that Wednesday? I can't believe it.' Hum. What do you
  suppose he means, where is it—'this a difficult time'?
STANITSIN: Well, the moneylenders are pressing pretty hard.
  He's sold his gold cigarette case and fancy watch.
OBLENSKY: Has he? 'You deserve only the best, not the worst.'
  Odd sentiment for a distinguished officer, don't you think?

52

He can't feel *that* sensitive about his extravagance, he's too reckless. Besides, as far as *he* knows, she's quite rich.

STANITSIN: Maybe he's just bored with her.

OBLENSKY: I don't think so, I'd say he's a passionate man, a bit callous too, and selfish, very, but there's something *in* all this.

STANITSIN: Come to that, the Countess sounds pretty convincing.

OBLENSKY: I hope not. All right.

(*He nods to* STANITSIN, *who opens the office door, and admits the* COUNTESS.)

Sit down. You seem to have lost your man.

COUNTESS: For the moment.

OBLENSKY: You mean you think you can get him back?

COUNTESS: Possibly.

OBLENSKY: Do you want to?

COUNTESS: What do you mean? I do what you tell me.

OBLENSKY: What's your assessment of Redl?

COUNTESS: Ambitious. Secretive. Violent. Vain. Extravagant. I expect you know as much as I do. You don't have to sleep with him to find that out.

OBLENSKY: Precisely. It doesn't seem to have added much to our total knowledge. However, patience. We're in no hurry. Captain Redl will be with us for a long time yet. Years and years. He'll probably improve with keeping. What's he doing with himself?

STANITSIN: What he says, working. Of course, he's hard up for the moment, but he'll——

OBLENSKY: Have you offered him money?

COUNTESS: Twice. He refused.

OBLENSKY: Won't take money from a woman. And I suppose you told him it didn't count between lovers?

COUNTESS: Naturally.

OBLENSKY: And there's no woman in Prague, nowhere, anyone? No one-night stands or twopenny standups?

STANITSIN: Nothing. He leaves his office in the War Building every day at 4.15, goes down to the café, has a coffee or two, reads all the foreign newspapers, has an early dinner, then goes back to his office and works till about ten, even eleven or twelve sometimes.

OBLENSKY: He *is* telling the truth.

STANITSIN: Occasionally he'll drop in for a drink somewhere on his way home or meet his friend Taussig for half an hour. More often than not he just sits alone.

OBLENSKY: Doing nothing?

STANITSIN: Just sitting. Looking.

OBLENSKY: Looking at what?

STANITSIN: I don't know. What *can* you look at from a café window? Other people, I suppose. Watch.

OBLENSKY: The Passing Show.

COUNTESS: Is there anything else?

OBLENSKY: No, my dear. Stanitsin will brief you.

(*She rises.*)

COUNTESS: Is it—may I have my letter?

OBLENSKY: I don't see why not.

(*Hands one to her.*)

COUNTESS: No, I meant his, to me.

OBLENSKY: I'm afraid that's for the File. Sorry. I can send you a copy. I wonder if he *will* write again. Don't forget to report, will you?

(STANITSIN *sees her out.* OBLENSKY *lights a cigarette.*)

FADE

SCENE 9

A café. REDL *sits alone at a table. Sitting a few tables away is a young man.* REDL *reads a paper. Throws away his cigar butt. Enter* TAUSSIG.

TAUSSIG: Ah, Redl, there you are. Sorry I'm late.

REDL: What will you have?

TAUSSIG: Don't think I'll bother. I promised to meet someone in ten minutes.

REDL: The one in the chorus at the Opera House?

TAUSSIG: That's the one.

54

REDL: Where?

TAUSSIG: She's taking me to her lodgings.

REDL: Before the performance? I hope it doesn't affect her voice. What's she like?

TAUSSIG: She rattles. Nice big girl.

REDL: They always are.

TAUSSIG: She's got a girl friend.

REDL: Thank you, no.

TAUSSIG: You seem awfully snobbish sometimes, Alfred.

REDL: Do I? I'm sorry. It's just that I'm not too keen on the opera. Are you going—afterwards?

TAUSSIG: What?

REDL: To the performance?

COUNTESS: Oh, yes, I suppose so. Your head must be hardened by all those ciphers. *Löhengrin*, I think. What's it like?

REDL: Boring.

TAUSSIG: So I believe. Oh, well. Sure you won't have supper after? She really is quite nice. They both are.

REDL: No, thank you, really.

TAUSSIG: Not going to Madame Heyse's do are you?

REDL: No. (*Pause.*)

TAUSSIG: Does that young man over there know you?

REDL: What young man?

TAUSSIG: Well, there's only one.

REDL: No. Why?

TAUSSIG: He's done nothing but stare at you. Oh, he's turned away now. Knows we're talking about him.

REDL: Prague's as bad as Vienna.

TAUSSIG: Keeps giggling to himself, as far as I can see.

REDL: Probably a cretin. Or a Czech who hates Austrian Army Officers. I can't face another of those evenings or dinners, here or anywhere. They all talk about each other. They're all clever and they're afraid of each other's cleverness. They're like beautiful, schooled performing dogs. Scrutinizing and listening for an unsteady foot. It's like hunting without the pig. Everyone sweats and whoops and rides together, and, at any time, any moment, the pig may turn out to be *you*. Stick!

TAUSSIG: Well, if I can't tempt you . . . Can I have one of your cigarettes? I say, the old case back, eh?

REDL: And the watch. Everything in fact.

TAUSSIG: Good for you. Make a killing?

REDL: I tipped my mare against Steinbauer's new gelding. Want a loan?

TAUSSIG: No thanks. The Countess isn't bothering you, is she?

REDL: I told you—no. We never got on. She was prickly and we were always awkward together. It was like talking to my sister. Who died, last week incidentally, consumption, and I can't say I thought about it more than ten minutes.

TAUSSIG: What will you do?

REDL: Now? Oh, have a quiet dinner. Go for a walk.

TAUSSIG: A walk? I don't know—well, if I can't persuade you. 'Bye.

(REDL *nods.* TAUSSIG *strides off. He picks up a paper, lights a new cigar. Presently the* YOUNG MAN *comes up to him.*)

YOUNG MAN: Excuse me, sir.

REDL: Well?

YOUNG MAN: May I glance at your paper?

REDL: If you wish. (*Irritated.*) The waiter will bring you one if you ask.

YOUNG MAN: I only want to see what's on at the Opera.

REDL: *Löhengrin.*

YOUNG MAN: Oh, thank you. No. I don't think I like Wagner much. Do you?

REDL: No. Now please go away.

(*The* YOUNG MAN *grins at him, and leans across to him, saying softly.*)

YOUNG MAN: I know what *you're* looking for.

(REDL *looks stricken. The* YOUNG MAN *walks away. He is almost out of sight when* REDL *runs after him.*)

REDL: You!

(REDL *grabs him with ferocious power by the neck.*)
What do you mean?

YOUNG MAN: Nothing! Let me go!

REDL: You pig, you little upstart pig. What did you mean?

YOUNG MAN: (*yells*). Let me go!

(Heads turn. REDL's *anger subsides into embarrassment. The* YOUNG MAN *walks away.* REDL *returns to his seat, lights his cigar, orders a drink from the* WAITER. *A Gipsy Band strikes up.)*

FADE

SCENE 10

A bare, darkened room. In it is a bed. On it two figures, not yet identifiable. A light is struck. A cigar end glows.

REDL's VOICE: Why wouldn't you keep the light on?
(*A figure leaves the bed and goes to a wash basin. Sound of water.*)
Um? Oh! Why did I wait—so long.
(REDL *lights a lamp beside the bed. By the washstand is the handsome form of a young* PRIVATE SOLDIER.)
Paul?

PAUL: Yes?

REDL: Why?

PAUL: I don't know. I just prefer the dark.

REDL: But why? My darling. You're so exquisite to look on—
You mean it's me?

PAUL: No. You look all right.

REDL: What is it, then? What are you dressing for?

PAUL: Got to get back to barracks, haven't I?

REDL: What's your unit?

PAUL: That'd be telling, wouldn't it?

REDL: Oh, come on, I can find out.

PAUL: Yes. General Staff and all that, isn't it?

REDL: Paul. What is it? What have I done? What are you opening the door for?
(PAUL *has opened the door. Four young* SOLDIERS *come in. They look at* REDL, *who knows instantly what will happen. He struggles violently at first, and for a while it looks as if they might have taken on too much. The young* SOLDIERS *in turn become amazed by* REDL's *vicious defence of himself, which is*

57

like an attack. All the while PAUL *dresses, pockets* REDL's *gold cigarette case, cigar case, watch and chain, gold crucifix, notes and change.* REDL *becomes a kicked, bloody heap on the floor. The* SOLDIERS *leave.* PAUL, *having dressed fully by now, helps* REDL *sit up against the bed, looks down at his bloody face.*)

PAUL: Don't be too upset, love. You'll get used to it.

(*Exit*)

CURTAIN

Act Two

SCENE 1

A Ballroom, Vienna. A winter evening in 1902. In the background a small, eccentrically dressed ORCHESTRA *plays. The light is not bright when the curtain goes up, except on the* SINGERS. *Concentrated silently, at first, anyway, are the* GUESTS, *among whom is* REDL, *one of the few not in fancy dress of some kind. However, he looks magnificent in his uniform and has put on his few decorations. He sprawls, listening thoughtfully to the* SINGER, *smoking one of his long black cigars. The* SINGER *is dressed in an eighteenth century dress which might allow the wearer to play Susanna in 'Figaro' or one of Mozart's ladies like* ZERLINA. *The* ORCHESTRA *plays very softly, the* SINGER *is restrained at this time, which is as well, because the voice is not adequate. However, it has enough sweetness in feeling to immediately invoke the pang of Mozart. Perhaps 'Vedrai Carino' or 'Batti, Batti' from 'Don Giovanni'. It ends quickly. Applause. Then a* MAN *dressed to play 'Figaro' appears, the lights become brighter, and the two go into the duet in the first scene of 'Figaro'. This should take no more than three minutes. It should be accepted at the beginning as the indifferent effort of a court opera house cast with amateurs, but not without charm and aplomb.*

The 'Figaro' in this case is a straight man. Presently, the 'Susanna' begins straight, then gradually cavorting, camping, and sending up the character, the audience, and Mozart as only someone in drag has the licence. The ballroom audience has been waiting for this, and is in ecstasy by the time it is over. Some call out 'do the Mad Scene'. Or 'Come Scoglio'. The 'Susanna', egged on, does a short parody of something like 'Come Scoglio', or 'Lucia' done in the headlong, take-it-on-the-chin manner.

This only takes a couple of minutes and should be quite funny. Anyhow, the ballroom audience apparently think so. Obviously, most of them have seen the performance before. There is a lot of giggling and even one scream during the ARIA, *which 'Susanna-Lucia' freezes with mock*

59

fury, and ends to great applause. 'Susanna' curtsies graciously. The lights in the room come up, the ORCHESTRA *strikes up and most of the guests dance. It is essential that it should only gradually be revealed to the audience that all the dancers and guests are men. The costumes, from all periods, should be in exquisite taste, both men's and women's, and those wearing them should look exotic and reasonably attractive, apart from an occasional grotesque. The music is gay, everyone chatters happily like a lot of birds and the atmosphere is generally relaxed and informal, in contrast to the somewhat stiff atmosphere at the ball in Act I. Among those dancing at present are* KUPFER, *dressed rather dashingly as* SCARAMOUCHE. KUNZ, *dancing one handed, with* MARIE ANTOINETTE, *looks rather good as* LORD NELSON. *The* WAITER ALBRECHT *from Scene 3, dressed as* COLUMBINE *with* KUPFER. FIGARO *dances with a* LADY GODIVA *in gold lamé jockstrap.* DOWNSTAGE, *holding court, is the host,* BARON VON EPP. *He is an imposing man with a rich flexible voice which he uses to effect. At present, he looks astonishingly striking with upswept hair, ospreys in pompadour feathers, a pearl and diamond dog collar at his neck, and a beautiful fan, as* QUEEN ALEXANDRA. *Again, it is essential that the costume should be in meticulous taste and worn elegantly and with natural confidence. Sitting beside him is someone dressed as a wimpled mediaeval lady, to be identified as* STEINBAUER. *Like* REDL *now, some years older.* REDL *is accompanied by* LIEUTENANT STEFAN KOVACS, *who is fixed in a mixture of amusement and embarrassment.* REDL *himself is quite cool, looking extremely dashing in his Colonel's uniform and decorations and close-cropped hair, staring very carefully around at all the guests, his eyes missing no one. He lights one of his long black cigars and joins the* BARON's *group, which includes* STEINBAUER, SUSANNA *and a ravishing* TSARINA.

NOTE: *At any drag ball as stylish and private as this one the guests can be seen to belong to entirely different and very distinct categories. 1. The paid bum boys whose annual occasion it is—they wait for it from one year to the next and spend between 3 and 6 months preparing an elaborate and possibly bizarre costume. This is the market place where in all probability they will manage to acquire a meal ticket for months ahead. They tend to either tremendously careful, totally feminine clothes—or the ultimate in revelation— e.g. Lady Godiva, except that he/she might think, instead of a gold*

*lamé jockstrap, that a gold chastity belt with a large and obvious
gold key on a chain round her/his neck, be better.*

*2. The discreet drag queens. Like the Baron/Queen Alexandra, and
the Tsarina—their clothes, specially made for the occasion by a
trusted dressmaker, as the night becomes wilder are usually found to
have a removable skirt revealing stockings, suspenders, jewelled
garters and diamond buckles on their shoes. But even despite this
mild strip tease, they still remain in absolutely perfect taste.*

*3. The more self-conscious rich queens, who, though in drag, tend to
masculine drag, and end up looking like lesbians. Someone tells me
they saw one once in marvellously cut black riding habit—frilled
white jabot and cuffs—long skirt and boots—top hat with veil. Also
in this category are the ones who go out of their way to turn themselves
into absolute grotesques, and quite often arrive in a gaggle. They
make a regal entry enjoying having their disguise penetrated or not
as the case may be. If, for instance, the theme of the ball were
theatrical they would probably choose to come as the witches from
Macbeth. But marvellously theatrically thought out in every detail.*

*4. Another category of rich, discreet queens, who don't want to
offend their host by making no effort at all but who baulk at dressing
up; for them full and impeccable evening dress with sash orders and
neck decorations and elaborately over made-up faces. They usually
look more frightening than any of the others—with middle-aged
decadent faces, painted like whores.*

*5. There are the men who positively dislike women and only put on
drag in order to traduce them and make them appear as odious,
immoral and unattractive as possible.*

*6. Finally, the ones who don't even make that effort but wear, like
Redl, full-dress uniform and decorations—or evening dress.*

*It's not inconceivable that some of the bum boys would dress as
pampered children.*

*Remember when they dance you don't find the male ones only
dancing with the female ones—but possibly a hussar with a man in
evening dress—or two men in evening dress together—or two
shepherdesses together.*

*In category 4 you would also be likely to find the made-up face—the
impeccable tails and white tie plus ropes of pearls and blazing
diamonds.*

61

BARON: Ah, Redl! How good to see you. Where have you been? You're always so busy. Everyone says you're in Counter Intelligence or something and you're frightfully grand now. I hope you're not spying on anyone here, Colonel. You know I won't have that sort of thing. I only give this ball once a year, and everyone invited is under the obligation of strictest confidence. No gossiping after. Otherwise you can all do as you like. Who's this?

REDL: May I introduce Lieutenant Stefan Kovacs—Baron Von Epp.

BARON: Very nice. Why are you both in mufti? You know my rule.

REDL: I wouldn't call the dress uniform of the Royal Imperial Army exactly mufti.

BARON: I'm surprised they let you in. I expect you know everyone, or will do.

REDL: It's rather astonishing. Almost everyone.

BARON: It's not astonishing at all. Colonel Redl, this is Captain Steinbauer—aren't you? Yes. She is.

REDL: (*to* STEINBAUER). Lemberg. Seventh Galician.

STEINBAUER: That's right. Siczynski.

REDL: Yes.

(*They look at each other. Sudden gratitude for the remembrance. And weariness, sadness. The* BARON *quickly dismisses the cloud.*)

BARON: And that's the Tsarina there. I don't know *who* she is exactly. A Russian spy I should think. Watch yourself, my dear, the Colonel eats a spy in bed every morning, don't you, Alfred? That's what they all tell me. It's even in the papers. And this is Ferdy.

(*He indicates* SUSANNA.)

Didn't you think he was divine?

REDL: Superb.

STEFAN: He really has a fine voice. I thought he was a real soprano at first.

(*They all look at him with some suspicion.*)

SUSANNA: What do you mean? I *am* a real soprano?

(*They all laugh.* STEFAN *feels he has blundered more than he has in fact.* REDL *chips in.*)

REDL: Isn't that Major Advocate Kunz?

BARON: Where? Oh, yes I see. Nelson, you mean. Doesn't he look marvellous. One arm and all! Wonder where he keeps it? He's my insurance.

REDL: What?

BARON: If there's ever any trouble, Kunz is my legal insurance. *Very* influential that one! She'll deal with anything that ever came up—Secret Police, anything, spies. No, spies is you, isn't it, Alfred, *you're* the spy-catcher, we'll leave any lovely little spies to you.

(*To* TSARINA.) Wait till he catches *you*. I daren't think *what* he'll do to you!

(*The* TSARINA *giggles*.)

Eh. Alfred? What do you do to naughty little spies?

REDL: (*bends down and grasps the* TSARINA's *ear lobe*). I tie them over the back of my mare, Kristina, on a leading rein, and beat them with my crop at a slow canter.

BARON: How delicious! Now, her earring's fallen off, you've excited her so!

(*The* TSARINA *retrieves her earring and smiles up in a sweet, friendly curious way at* REDL, *who smiles back, touched by an instant, simple, affectionate spirit. He turns to* STEFAN, *who has looked away. Quickly noted by the* BARON.)

BARON: I haven't seen your Lieutenant Kovacs before, Alfred.

REDL: He's only just graduated from the War School.

BARON: All that studying and hardening the body and noontide heat and sweating, and horses! You all look quite beautiful, well, some of you, but I hate to think of you in a war. A real war.

(*A* SHEPHERDESS *serves champagne*.)

Oh, come along, come along. No one's drinking half enough yet. Alfred!

(REDL *downs a glass. He looks flushed and suddenly relaxed*.)

And another! You're behind the rest of us. And a good place for you, said someone.

(REDL *takes another. Hands one to* STEFAN.)

And Ferdy, you have some more. Good for the voice. Bit strained tonight, dear. I want you to do 'Una Donna A Quindici Anni'.

63

FERDY: Don't think I can.

BARON: You can do *anything*. Practically. (*To* REDL.) He has hair on his instep—like a goat. Show them. Oh, well . . . Where have you two come from? The Lieutenant looks rather glum.

REDL: We were at the Hofburg for an hour or two.

BARON: No wonder he looks glum. Come along! Drink up, Lieutenant. I can't have anyone sober at my party. (*To* REDL.) I suppose you *had* to go, being so powerful now and impressive.

REDL: Oh, come along.

BARON: No, I hear it's quite true. (*To* STEINBAUER.) You remember the Colonel then?

STEINBAUER: Years ago. I always knew he'd make a brilliant officer. We all did. Congratulations, Colonel! (*Raises glass—talks to* TSARINA.)

BARON: Mind your wimple. She gets drunk too easily, that one. Which is probably why she's still only a humble captain in number seventy-seven. (*Out of* STEFAN's *hearing.*) Are you sure your friend wouldn't rather be back at the Hofburg?

REDL: He'll be all right. Try and leave him alone.

BARON: I can't leave anyone *that* pretty alone. Do you want the Tsarina? She's Kunz's really, but she's pretty available. (*Pause.* REDL *considers.*) And Kunz isn't the kind who makes scenes. He doesn't care . . . He's a bit cold too. (STEFAN *hears the last of this.*)

STEFAN: Did you say Kunz? Isn't a man like that taking a bit of a risk?

BARON: Aren't we all?

STEFAN: Yes. But for someone . . .

BARON: We are none of us safe. This——
(*He sweeps his fan round the ballroom.*)
is the celebration of the individual against the rest, the us's and the them's, the free and the constricted, the gay and the dreary, the lonely and the mob, the little Tsarina there and the Emperor Francis Joseph.
(*They laugh.*)
Tell your friend it's so, Alfred.

REDL: Oh, I agree.

STEFAN: (*To* REDL.) Forgive me, I feel I'm unwanted.

BARON: Nonsense. You're *wanted*. Tell him not to be a silly, solemn boy, Alfred.

(REDL *squeezes the boy's arm and laughs. The* BARON *refills* STEFAN's *glass.*)

Actually, Kunz is an odd one. He seems to take appalling risks, but he knows the right people everywhere and anywhere, and he'd sell anyone, and I know him. He's my first cousin. He'd do it to me.

STEFAN: Blood not thicker than water?

BARON: His blood is thinner than anything, my dear.

FERDY: Darling! She wants to know——

BARON: What is it? I'm talking.

FERDY: Are you really a Baron?

(*The* TSARINA *giggles.*)

BARON: Tell her she'll find out if she's not careful.

TSARINA: (*to* FERDY.) Are you the Baroness then?

FERDY: (*nods*). Oh. I let him. He fancies himself chasing the ladies, but he's just the same as I am. Nothing more at all.

TSARINA: What about the Lieutenant?

FERDY: Oh, I should think so. Either too stupid to know it, or hasn't woken up to it yet.

TSARINA: Or doesn't want to wake up to it. Looks a bit dreary.

FERDY: Do you fancy him? You'll have the Colonel after you. You'll be shot down.

(*While this duet has gone on, the* BARON, STEFAN *and* REDL *have drawn away from the* GIRLS *into their own conversation. Some class division here too.*)

BARON: Vienna is so dull! All that Spanish gloom at the Hofburg gets in everywhere, like the moth.

FERDY: (*calls out*). *You* need moth balls! (*Collapse.*)

BARON: The Viennese gull themselves they're gay, but they're just stiff-jointed aristocrats like puppets, grubbing little tradesmen or Jews and chambermaids making a lot of one-two-three noises all the time. Secretly, they're feeling utterly thwarted and empty. The bourgeoisie daren't enjoy themselves except at someone else's expense or misfortune.

And all those cavorting, clever Jews are even more depressing, pretending to be generous—and *entirely* unspontaneous. Hungarians, they're gay, perhaps that's because they're quite selfish and pig-headed. Kovacs: oh, dear, are you Hungarian? Well, never mind, that's me again I'm afraid, speak first, think afterwards——

REDL: No, Baron, you're ahead of everyone.

BARON: Only wish I were. Poles are fairly gay. You're Polish or something, aren't you, Alfred? And somehow they're less *common* than Russians. Serbs are impossible, of course, savage, untrustworthy, worse than Hungarians, infidels in every sense. I think your friend despises me because I'm such a snob. What is your father, Lieutenant?

STEFAN: A chef at the Volksgarten Restaurant.

BARON: And do you think I'm a snob?

STEFAN: You appear to be.

BARON: Well, of course, I am. Alfred will tell you how much. However, I'm also a gentleman, which is preferable to being one of our dear Burgomaster Lueger's mob. Taste, a silk shirt, a perfumed hand, an ancient Greek ring are things that come from a way not only of thinking but of being. They can add up to a man. (*To* STEFAN.) Would you like to walk on the terrace? The view is rather remarkable on an evening like this.

STEFAN: Alfred?

BARON: We'll join you. Or come back soon. I want to ask the Colonel's advice. About some espionage.

(STEFAN *bows and leaves through the high central glass doors.*)
Well, my dear friend. And how are you? You're prosperous I hear.

REDL: I had a small legacy.

BARON: Good. A man like you knows what money's for. And you *look* so well. Forgive me for sending the boy away for a moment.

REDL: That's all right. He'll find something to amuse him.

BARON: Would it be impertinent to ask: you're not wasting your time there are you?

REDL: It would.

66

BARON: What? Oh, I see. Quite right. Only I admire you, Redl. So does everyone else. You're a credit to—everyone. I just want you to succeed in everything you undertake.

REDL: Thank you.

(KUNZ *comes over with his partner,* MARIE ANTOINETTE.)

BARON: Jaroslaw! Have some champagne.

KUNZ: Thank you.

BARON: And let me introduce Colonel Redl—Major Advocate Kunz.

(*They salute each other appropriately.*)

FERDY: Colonel! Would you come over here a minute. The Tsarina wants to give herself up.

(TSARINA *screams.*)

She says, she says she wants to confess!

(*The* TSARINA *pulls off* FERDY'*s wig and smacks him with it.* REDL *smiles and excuses himself to* KUNZ.)

BARON: Ferdy! That's naughty! The Colonel was talking to Major Kunz.

FERDY: No, he wasn't. Here!

(*He places* REDL *beside him and the* TSARINA.)

We've been talking to you. (*To* BARON.) *You* don't listen! It's secret.

(*The* BARON *smiles happily.*)

BARON: Alfred *knows* all the secrets. It's his job.

(FERDY *and the* TSARINA *conduct a whispered conversation with* REDL *for a while. He is drinking freely now, and is excited and enjoying himself. The* BARON *turns to* KUNZ.)

Don't you think my little Ferdy's brilliant? He'd make an adorable 'Cherubino'.

KUNZ: I think he's prettier as 'Susanna'.

BARON: Perhaps. He made that costume himself. Up half the night.

KUNZ: Did you see who I came with?

BARON: No. Why?

KUNZ: Good. I thought I'd spice your party a bit this year.

BARON: What have you done?

KUNZ: I brought a woman.

(*The* BARON *looks astonished. Then yelps with laughter.*)

67

BARON: Oh, *what* a good idea! What a *stroke!* Where is she?
(*He looks around.*)

KUNZ: That's the point. Later on, we'll all have to guess.

BARON: And find out! Marvellous! We'll unmask her. I'll offer a prize to the man who strips her.

KUNZ: And, I think, a punishment for anyone who is mistaken.

BARON: Exactly. What fun! I do enjoy these things. I wish we could have one every month. I'm so glad you liked Ferdy.

KUNZ: How long is it now?

BARON: Three years.

KUNZ: Long time.

BARON: For me. Let's be honest, for nearly all of us. *And* women. No, three years is a big bite out of a lifetime when you never know when it may come to an end, or what you may have missed. But he's very kind. He's still young. But his growing old gnaws at me a bit, you know. Not that he still doesn't look pretty good in the raw. Oh, he does. But about me, he doesn't mind at all.

KUNZ: Who's the little flower with Redl?

BARON: No idea. *Something's* made her wilt. They've both just come from the Hofball.

KUNZ: So have I.

BARON: Of course. Poor you. And with your lady escort. I wonder if I'll spot her.
(*He stares around.*)
That's her!

KUNZ: That is the doorman at the Klomser Hotel.

BARON: Oh! I see I'm not going to. What on earth made you go to the Hofball?

KUNZ: I thought it might be amusing to go there first.
(KUNZ *nods at* REDL, *who is being captivated by* FERDY, and starting to get recurring fits of giggles.)
Look at the Colonel.

BARON: (*pleased*). He's enjoying himself.

KUNZ: I've never seen him like that before.

BARON: How many people have seen *you*? He's letting his hair down. What's left of it. It's starting to go. I noticed just now. He's a handsome devil.

68

KUNZ: Very.

BARON: And a brilliant officer, they say. Suppose you should be if you're at the top in counter espionage.

KUNZ: Preferably. He works morning and night.

BARON: He's only a railway clerk's son, did you know? So I suppose he's had to. Work, I mean. But he plays too. Look at him.

(REDL *and* FERDY *are swopping stories and giggling intermittently and furiously.* REDL *tries to light another cigar, but he can scarcely get it going. The* TSARINA *watches blankly and happily.*)
He told me once how hard he'd tried to change.

KUNZ: Hey, you! Little Shepherdess!
(*He takes a drink from a blushing* SHEPHERDESS.)
Beautiful. Yes?

BARON: Tried everything, apparently. Resolutions, vows, religion, medical advice, self-exhaustion. Used to flog a dozen horses into the ground in a day. And then gardening, if you please, fencing and all those studies they do, you do, of course—military history, ciphers, telegraphy, campaigns, he knows, hundreds of them, by heart. He knows his German literature, speaks superb French and Russian, Italian, Polish, Czech *and* Turkish if you please.

KUNZ: Not bad for a Ruthenian railway clerk.

BARON: As you say. Oh, take your eye of Redl. He's not after the Tsarina. Or Ferdy. Is he? No, I don't think so. He's just being himself for once. Don't you think we should all form an Empire of our own?

KUNZ: What's that?

BARON: Well, instead of all joining together, you know, one Empire of sixty million Germans, like they're always going on about. What about an Empire of *us*. Ex million queens.

KUNZ: Who would there be?

BARON: Well, you and me for a start. I'd be Minister of Culture, I think. Redl could catch any spies, *women* spies. And you could do what you liked.

KUNZ: And who else?

BARON: Not Jews I think. They're the least queer in my

opinion. Their mothers won't let them. Germans,
Prussians, they're *very* queer. All that duelling. Poles, not
so much.

KUNZ: Italians?

BARON: No, they're like women, only better, women con brio.
Hungarians are just goats, of course, but some are quite
nice. French: too spry to let life play a trick on *them*.

KUNZ: What about the English?

BARON: Next, after the Germans.

KUNZ: I agree with that. Queen Victoria was quite clearly a
man.

BARON: But *she* was a German, wasn't she?

KUNZ: Ah, yes. Still, you're right about the English.

BARON: I believe Redl has an Eton straw boater hanging over his
bed as a trophy. They say it belongs to the younger son of the
British Ambassador.

(*Pause.*)

How's that son of yours?

(KUNZ *looks immediately on guard.*)

I was only asking.

KUNZ: He's well.

BARON: I'm sorry. It must be difficult. If people *will* get married.

KUNZ: Well, *I* did.

BARON: The boy knows nothing?

KUNZ: Nothing.

BARON: His mother hasn't——

KUNZ: No. And she won't.

BARON: Why not? Doesn't she——

KUNZ: She pretends.

BARON: Ah! They *do*. And the boy?

KUNZ: *He's* all right, if that's what you mean.

BARON: You mean you're *not* all right?

KUNZ: Who knows? Is this Redl's flower?

(STEFAN *approaches.*)

BARON: Yes. My dear boy, you must meet the Major Advocate
Kunz. Lieutenant—I'm sorry——?

STEFAN: Kovacs.

(*They salute.*)

BARON: Hungarian. Did you enjoy the terrace? I knew you
would. Oh, thank heaven the music's stopped. Alfred's been
having the giggles with little Ferdy while you've been away.
Do have another glass, dear boy.

(REDL *and* FERDY *stand up, giggling helplessly. The others
listen.*)

FERDY: And the manager, said, he said to me: we don't allow
ladies in here, in here without male escorts.

(REDL *doubles up.*)

And, so I pointed at the Baron and said, what do you think
he is!

(REDL *falls on the* TSARINA *who squeals.*)

KUNZ: (*to* STEFAN). Is this your first visit to this kind of thing?

STEFAN: Yes, sir.

BARON: Oh, don't call him sir. Just because he's dressed as
Nelson. He's only an old Army lawyer. I must say you look
very fine with that black patch. We must find a Lady
Hamilton for him before the evening's out, mustn't we? I
was saying, where do you keep your arm?

(KUNZ *leaves it out of his tunic, and stretches it.*)

Ah, there it is, you see?

KUNZ: That's better.

BARON: You danced very well, all the same.

KUNZ: (*to* STEFAN). Would you care to?

(STEFAN *is slightly confused for a moment.*)

STEFAN: Thank you, I'm a bit hot.

BARON: Must be cold on that terrace.

KUNZ: You see, this is a place for people to come together. People
who are very often in their everyday lives, rather lonely and
even miserable and feel hunted. As if they had a spy catcher
like the Colonel on their heels.

STEFAN: Of course. I understand that.

KUNZ: And, because of the Baron's panache and generosity—and,
let's be frank, recklessness——

BARON: Look's who's talking——

KUNZ: They come together and become something else. Like
sinners in a church.

(FERDY *stands up.*)

71

LADY GODIVA: Two monks in the street.

TSARINA: I *like* monks.

LADY GODIVA: Two monks. Walking in the street. One's saying his rosary to himself. The other passes by as he's saying 'Hail Mary'. And the other stops and says: 'Hullo, Ursula.'

(REDL *collapses. So does* FERDY. *Then recovers professionally. The others watch, and some of the dancers too, including* KUPFER *and* ALBRECHT-COLUMBINE, *and* FIGARO *and* LADY GODIVA. *General laughter. The* BARON *is pleased.* FERDY *sits back next to* REDL *and they both drink and giggle together, mostly at nothing, until later in the scene when* REDL *takes in* KUPFER *and becomes hostile: to* KUPFER, *drunkenness and himself.*

KUNZ: You're not enjoying yourself much. (*Small pause.*) Are you?

(STEFAN *blushes.*)

STEFAN: Not at all.

KUNZ: You mustn't judge the world at carnival time. There is such a thing, such a contract, such a bond as marriage——

BARON: You should know, poor soul.

KUNZ: And there is friendship, comradeship. In the midst of all this, I ask you not to sneer, or I will beat your sanctimonious head in——

BARON: Jaroslaw——

KUNZ: Aristotle, if you've heard of him.

STEFAN: I have——

BARON: Please; take no notice . . .

KUNZ: I'm glad to hear it. Says it can be either good, or pleasant or useful. Which is true, but not always. But he also says it lasts in such men only, only as long as they keep their goodness. And goodness, unfortunately, Lieutenant, does not last.

STEFAN: No?

KUNZ: No. And don't be insolent.

STEFAN: Then don't be offensive.

BARON: Tempers, darlings, tempers!

KUNZ: It seldom lasts shall we say? But then such men are rare, anyway.

(*The other guests gather round, and listen, and begin to take part. During this sequence,* REDL *sobers up and stiffens.*)

72

KUPFER: Good evening, Colonel Redl.

REDL: I don't . . .

KUPFER: *Now* you do . . .

BARON: *Everyone!* Met *everyone* before. (*To* ALBRECHT.)

KUPFER: Kupfer. Major Kupfer, sir. General Staff. Ninth Corps. Prague.

REDL: Prague, Prague . . . This is Vienna. What are you doing here?

KUPFER: Same as you, sir. On leave.

REDL: *I'm* not on leave.

KUPFER: I didn't necessarily mean literally——

REDL: You'll remember Steinbauer then?

KUPFER: Of course.

(*He greets the wimpled* STEINBAUER *casually*.)

It was a blow about Siczynski. (*Pause*.) Wasn't it?

REDL: Was it?

KUPFER: Wasn't he a particular friend of yours?

REDL: I scarcely knew him. We neither of us did . . .

KUPFER: Why did you agree to be his second? It wasn't a very correct thing for such a correct officer as you to be doing.

REDL: I thought he should have support . . . No one liked him.

KUPFER: But *you've* always been popular, Colonel.

REDL: Are you being . . . because if so . . .

KUPFER: You only have my admiration, Colonel. With all the advantages I was born with, I only wish I—could—ever go—so far. You seemed to be having an entertaining time just there, Colonel. Please don't let me——

FERDY: Don't you think he's beautiful? I adore it when he screws his monocle in his eye.

(REDL *doesn't think this at all funny, though the* BARON *and* KUNZ *are pleased, and, of course,* KUPFER. REDL *stands more erect than ever, and lights up a fresh cigar, grabbing a glass from the passing* SHEPHERDESS.)

REDL: Hey, you! Fräulein!

FERDY: Have you heard about that extraordinary Dr. Schoepfer?

KUPFER: No. Who is he?

FERDY: Don't you know? My dear, he sounds divine! The Tsarina went there last night.

STEINBAUER: What does he do?

FERDY: Just talks, my dear, for *hours*. Not a smile. Medical do's and all that, but, if you say you're a student, you can get in.

KUPFER: What's he talk about?

FERDY: Why, *us*. He sounds an absolute scream. Can't stop talking about it.

REDL: Us? Speak for yourself.

BARON: What's he say then, Ferdy?

FERDY: Oh, that we're all demented something, something cox on the end, darling.

(*Laughter*.)

LADY GODIVA: Well, he's right, of course.

FERDY: That we're all potential criminals, and some of us should even be castrated.

(*Screams*.)

And that we're a warning symptom of the crisis in, oh, civilization, and the decline in Christian whatnots.

BARON: Oh, and he goes on about marriage and the family being the basis of the Empire, and *we* must be rooted out. *She* says he's a scream.

(*They look at the* TSARINA, *who nods, giggles and goes crimson*.)

MARIE ANTOINETTE: Is he a Jew?

FERDY: But, of course, darling! She says he looks like Shylock's mother.

KUPFER: But who is he?

KUNZ: A neurologist, I believe. Nerves.

BARON: Well, I'm sure he'd get on mine.

KUNZ: I think he's one of those people who insist they can penetrate the inner secrets of your own nature.

BARON: I understand the inner secrets of my nature perfectly well. I don't admire them, but I do know them, anyway better than this Dr. Schoepfer.

FERDY: Silly mare!

BARON: And I'm quite happy as I am, I'm no criminal, thank you, and I don't corrupt anything that isn't already quite clearly corrupt, like this ghastly city. On the contrary, I bring style, wit, pleasure, energy and good humour to it that it wouldn't otherwise have.

74

KUPFER: Well said, Baron.

BARON: More drinks, everyone! And music! (*To* MUSICIANS.)

ALBRECHT: I went to a doctor once, and he just said 'pull your socks
up'. Do you know what he told me to do? Go into the Army!
(*Shrieks.*) And find yourself a nice girl. Get married. So:
naturally, I went into the Army. Artillery. In the second week
I'd been seduced by the Corporal of Horse *and* a sub-lieutenant.

BARON: Oh, I went to a doctor like a silly thing when I was a
student. He just looked very agitated and told me there was
nothing he could do and to go away. A few years later I heard
he'd cut his throat . . .

MARIE ANTOINETTE: I plucked up courage to tell *our* family
doctor, and I said I'd like to be sent away to some special
clinic in Vienna . . . Well, I thought he was going to go
raving mad. Vienna, he said, Vienna, *you* want to go to
Vienna. I'll send you to hell. You'll find all you want *there*,
you quivering, scheming little sissy!

ALBRECHT: When I first came to Vienna, it seemed like paradise,
but now I do get a bit bored. Not here, of course, Baron. But
you know what I mean. Same tired old exhibits. Nothing
new ever seems to come in.

TSARINA: (*now sitting on the* BARON'*s knee shyly*). I remember the
first time a man tickled the palm of my hand with his middle
finger, when we shook hands, and then later he told me what
he was. I was very religious then, and I thought he was
wicked. I really did at the time.

KUNZ: Perhaps you were right.

LADY GODIVA: *I* went to our priest. He quoted Aquinas and
said anything that was against nature was against God . . .
He always kept an eye on me afterwards, always pulling me
up and asking me questions.

STEINBAUER: *My* priest said: you *can't* be like that. You're a
soldier, a man of courage and honour and virtue. Your
uniform itself embodies the glory of the Empire and the
Church. I worshipped Radetzky at the time, and he knew it.
So he said do you think someone like Radetzky could have
ever been like that? I didn't know about Julius Caesar and
Alexander then.

75

FIGARO: (*to* REDL, *who is like a frozen ox*). I hate these screamers, don't you?

LADY GODIVA: I used to go to the priest after I'd confessed I was in love with Fritz. Then I used to lie like crazy about it, and say nothing was happening, although we were having sex regularly. And he'd give me absolution and say, 'It may not take on immediately——'
(*Laughter.*)

LADY GODIVA: If Fritz just moved his little finger at me, I'd go back. Then he went with a girl suddenly and got married. When she was pregnant, we had beers together, and he pinched my arm and kissed me. Then he laughed and said: You know what you are, find someone else the same . . . But he laughed . . .

FERDY: I should think so, you soppy little thing.
(FERDY *is bored with all this and wants attention.*)
I only went to a doctor once and he just said take more exercise, dear. So I did.
(*He executes a skilful entrechat to general amusement till* REDL *strikes him hard across the face, knocking him down right into the other guests. The boy is stunned by the force of it. Silence.*)

REDL: Baron—forgive me.
(*He clicks his heels and goes, followed presently by* STEFAN *in silence. Then the* BARON *booms out over a few 'Wells!', etc.*)

BARON: Someone pick up poor Ferdy. You silly boy! I knew you shouldn't have flirted with Colonel Redl. He's a dangerous man. Are you better? There now! Come along, everybody, that's quite enough melodrama. On with the ball—I suppose——
(*They reassemble. Lights lower. And they hear the spirit of Mozart as* FERDY *sings, not without some sweetness, 'Vedrai Carino' or 'Batti, Batti'. Or something similar which is tolerably within his range.*)

FADE

SCENE 2

Lecture Room. Rostrum. A glass of water. DR. SCHOEPFER *is speaking.*

SCHOEPFER: The *evasion*, naturally, of responsibility . . . For instance in enjoying the physical sensations of the body without any reference to the responsibilities involved in the relationship. Or, indeed, to society or any beliefs, such as a belief in God. They can never, in their ignorance, some men say folly, in their infirmity, never attain that complete love, the love that only is possible between men and women, whose shared interests . . .
(*There is a suppressed giggle.*)
. . . whose shared interests include the blessed gift of children and grandchildren which alone, I think, most people would agree even today, which alone gives a grand and enduring purpose to sexual congress.
(*He drinks from the glass of water.*)
Now, gentlemen: these traits are caused by regression to the phallic stage of libido development, and can be traced to what is in fact a flight from incest . . .

FADE

SCENE 3

A hill clearing outside Dresden, surrounded by fir trees. Cold winter. OBLENSKY *is warmly wrapped up in his greatcoat, sitting on a tree trunk smoking a cigarette.* STANITSIN *stands beside him.*

STANITSIN: Here he comes.
OBLENSKY: To the minute. As you'd expect. You'd better give me the file. Oh, just a minute, have you got the parcel I asked for?
(STANITSIN *nods.*)

77

It wasn't easy this week getting in. The boy Kovacs is staying there while he's commanding this exercise.

(REDL *enters, smoking a cigar. He looks cool and sure of himself.*)

REDL: Mr. Smith?

OBLENSKY: Yes, indeed. Rather *this* is Mr. Smith.

REDL: Look, I haven't time to waste fooling about——

OBLENSKY: Quite. You got our message, and, blessedly, you are here, Colonel Redl.

REDL: And who the devil are you?

OBLENSKY: Colonel Oblensky.

REDL: Oblensky . . .

(OBLENSKY *waits for the effect to take, and goes on.*)

OBLENSKY: It won't take you long, Colonel. I know your regiment is waiting for you . . . loosely speaking. I have a file here, which I would like to acquaint you with briefly. Would you care to sit down?

(REDL *doesn't move.*)

Just a matter of minutes. I have no anxiety about you reaching for your revolver to shoot either of us. I know you will realize that all this file is duplicated both in Warsaw *and* St. Petersburg. What I do beg of you is to pause before you think of turning it on yourself. I think we can find a satisfactory, and probably long-term arrangement which will work out quite well for all of us, and no trouble.

REDL: (*recovering, coldly*). May I see?

OBLENSKY: Naturally, oh, this is Lieutenant Stanitsin.

(STANITSIN *bows.*)

REDL: Mr. Smith?

STANITSIN: My pen name, sir.

(REDL *puts out his hand impatiently for the file.*
OBLENSKY *hands him the contents in batches. They watch* REDL *flip through, stone faced.*)

REDL: Mess bills in Lemberg! Eighteen eighty-nine! Tailors' bills, jeweller's, stables, coachbuilders, tobacconists. What *is* all this? They're just bills.

OBLENSKY: Rather unusual bills for a young officer of no independent means.

REDL: I have an uncle——

OBLENSKY: You have no uncle, Colonel. Two brothers only. Both happily married—and penniless.

(*Hands him another bill.*)

Cartiers. One gold cigarette case inscribed 'to dearest Stefan with love, Alfred'.

REDL: My nephew.

(OBLENSKY *hasn't the heart to smile at this.* REDL's *immediate humiliation is so evident.*)

OBLENSKY: Your bank statements from the Austro-Hungarian Bank in both Vienna and Prague for the month of February.

(REDL *hardly looks at them. Pause.*)

REDL: Well?

OBLENSKY: I'm sorry, Colonel. We'll soon get this over. One letter, date, February 17th 1901. 'My darling, don't be angry. When I make no sign, you know or should know, that I love you. Please see me again. All I long for is to lie beside you, nothing else. I don't know what to do to kill the time before I see you again, and watch you, how I can do something to pass the time.'

REDL: It is no crime to write a love letter, Colonel, even if it isn't in the style of Pushkin.

OBLENSKY: The style's tolerable enough for a man in love . . . But this letter is not addressed to a woman.

REDL: There's no name on it.

OBLENSKY: There is on the envelope.

REDL: *Not* very convincing, Colonel.

OBLENSKY: Very well. Those—if you'd just glance through them quickly—are signed affidavits from——

(REDL *won't look at them. He has mustered himself wonderfully. He feels the chance of a small hope.*)

(*Politely, casually*). The page at the Grand Hotel, a musician at the Volksgarten—this is only the last six weeks, you understand—a waiter at Sacher's, a Corporal in the Seventh Corps in Prague, a boatman in Vienna, a pastry cook, a compositor on the 'Deutsches Volksblatt' and a *reporter* on the 'Neue Freie Press'. (*Pause.*) One right-wing paper, one liberal, eh?

(REDL *puffs on his cigar.*)

REDL: (*slowly*). Whores. Bribed, perjuring whores.

OBLENSKY: Yes. Against the word of a distinguished officer in the Royal Imperial Army . . . Oh, dear . . . Stanitsin. Photographs . . .

(STANITSIN *hands a bundle of large photographs to* REDL *who looks at the first four or five. Then he hands them back. Pause. He sits on another trunk and slowly puts his face in his hands.*) Offer the Colonel some brandy.

(STANITSIN *offers him a flask, which he drinks from.*)

I think *I'll* have some, Stanitsin. Now that's all over, let us all have some. Forgive me, Colonel. Now: time is short for us. What you decide to do is up to you. There are three courses open to you. One we have mentioned. The second is to leave the Army. The third is to remain in the Army and continue with your brilliant career. Do you know what Russia spent on espionage last year, Colonel? Nine million roubles. Nine. This year it will be even more. What do your people spend? Half? No, I've watched you for more than ten years, and you'd be surprised probably, or perhaps I'm wrong, about how much I know about the kind of man you are. What can you do? Change your way of life? It's getting desperate already, isn't it? You don't know which way to turn, you're up to your eye-balls in debts. What could you do? Get thrown out, exposed for everything you are, or what the world would say you are. Would you, do you think, *could* you change your way of life, what else do you want after all these years, what would you do at your age, go back to base and become a waiter or a washer up, sit all alone in cafés again constantly *watching*? What are you fit for?

(*His tone relaxes.*)

The same as me, my dear friend, the same as me, and very good indeed you are at it, soldiering, war and treachery, or the treachery that leads to wars. The game. It's a fine one. And no one's better at it in Europe than me—at the moment. (*Smiles.*) Heavy turnover sometimes. Tell me, do none of your brother officers know or suspect?

REDL: Kovacs, Kupfer, Steinbauer . . . No.

OBLENSKY: And Kunz? Kunz's only real indiscretion is the
Baron's annual ball, and he could always say he went as a
relation or even as a tourist even though it's hardly
respectable. We've never caught him out in all these years,
have we, Stanitsin? He does . . . doesn't he . . .?
REDL: I assume so.
OBLENSKY: The other two, Steinbauer and Kupfer, well, they
seem to have left wormcasts all over Europe, so they're no
threat to you. And Kovacs, he's only—been—with *you*,
hasn't he?
REDL: Yes.
OBLENSKY: Sure?
REDL: (*wryly*). Colonel Oblensky, I may find myself here before
you, in this position, but I remind you that I *am* an officer
in the Austrian Chief of Staff's Counter Espionage
Department. *I* know how to interrogate myself. The
answer's yes.
(OBLENSKY *smiles*.)
OBLENSKY: Oh, I'm the last to under-estimate you, Colonel. Last
report from General Staff Headquarters January 5th:
'supremely capable, learned, intuitive and precise in
command, tactful, excellent manners.' And now your
handling of the corps exercise on Monday: 'He is
uncommonly striking. Both as a battalion and regimental
commander.' And there's your Regiment, the 77th Infantry.
Didn't the Emperor call it 'my beautiful Seventy Seventh'.
Oh, you certainly chose the right career, Colonel. Cigarette?
I think the really interesting thing about you, Redl, is that
you yourself are really properly aware of your own
distinction—as you should be. If you ever do feel any shame
for what you are, you don't accept it like a simpleton, you
heave it off, like a horse that's fallen on you. And the result
is, I suppose what they mean by that splendid Viennese style.
Ah, the time, yes, we must be going. Give the Colonel his
package.
(STANITSIN *does so*.)
REDL: Is that all?
OBLENSKY: You must be returning to the regiment, Colonel.

REDL: What's this?

OBLENSKY: Mr. Smith will contact you when you've had a few
days to rest and recover generally. The package contains
seven thousand kronen in notes . . . Far more than *you* pay,
Colonel.

(REDL *puts it in his pocket slowly, collects himself, and bows.*)

Goodbye, Colonel. I don't suppose we shall meet again for a
long time—if ever . . . It *is* a little risky, even for you, isn't
it?

(*He laughs, full of good humour.*)

Oh, Stanitsin, the parcel.

(*He hands a paper bag to* REDL, *who, puzzled, takes from it an
Etonian straw boater.*)

Perhaps you should return it to the British Ambassador.

(*He laughs heartily.*)

Forgive me, Colonel, but I do have a very clumsy, clumsy
sense of humour sometimes. No, always!

(STANITSIN *smiles and goes out. The two men watch him.
Presently they hear his laughter floating back through the woods.*)

CURTAIN

Act Three

SCENE 1

REDL's *apartment in Vienna. Baroque, luxurious. It is late afternoon, the curtains are drawn, the light comes through them and two figures can just be seen in bed. One is* REDL *who appears to be asleep. The other, the figure of a* YOUNG MAN, *is getting up very quietly, almost stealthily, and dressing. There is a rattle of coins and jewellery.*

REDL: Don't take my cigarette case, will you? *Or* my watch.
> (*The boy hesitates.*)
> There's plenty of change. Take that. Go on. Now you'd better . . . hurry back.
> (*The boy slips out quickly, expertly.* REDL *sits up and lights a cigar. He gets up and puts on a beautiful dressing gown. Presently* KUPFER *comes in.*)
> Who's that? Oh, you? Why don't you knock?

KUPFER: I knew you were alone.

REDL: What's the time?

KUPFER: Four. Shall I open the shutters?
> (*He does so.* REDL *shrinks a little.*)

REDL: That's enough.

KUPFER: The sun's quite hot.
> (*He sits in an armchair by the window.*)
> I waited. Till your little friend left.

REDL: Very courteous. Well?

KUPFER: I've news.

REDL: Bad, no doubt.

KUPFER: Afraid so.

REDL: Out with it.

KUPFER: Stefan was married secretly this morning.
> (*Pause.*) To the Countess Delyanoff.

83

(*Pause.*)

REDL: Naturally. The bitch . . .Does she want to see me?

KUPFER: Why, yes—she's waiting.

REDL: Well, go and get her. And then go away.

(KUPFER *turns.*)

No. Wait outside.

(KUPFER *goes and* REDL *smokes his cigar, looking out of the window. Soon the* COUNTESS *enters.*)

COUNTESS: Alfred?

REDL: So: you pulled it off.

COUNTESS: Alfred. We've endured all of that. Can't we——

REDL: No. What's he doing, marrying *you?*

COUNTESS: He loves me. No more . . .

REDL: I suppose you're calving.

COUNTESS: I'm having his child, Alfred.

REDL: I knew it! Knew it!

COUNTESS: He *would* have married me. He was disgusted by your behaviour.

REDL: Oh?

COUNTESS: You must admit, Alfred, telling him I was Jewish wasn't very subtle—for *you.*

REDL: Well, you are, aren't you? And I don't believe you'd told him.

COUNTESS: No, I hadn't. But my *not* telling him was cowardly, not vulgar, like yours *was.* You surprise me, Alfred.

REDL: And he'll have to resign his commission as he's no means?

COUNTESS: He wants to go into journalism.

REDL: And become a politician.

COUNTESS: Alfred, we had such feeling for each other once.

REDL: I didn't, you Jewish prig, you whited sepulchre, does he know what you really are, apart from a whore, a whoring spy?

COUNTESS: No. He doesn't. No one knows. Except you. It's extraordinary you should have kept it a secret, but I don't expect you to behave differently now.

REDL: Don't count on it . . . You little Jewish spy——

COUNTESS: I'm not, not now, Alfred, you know . . . it was my husband, when he was alive——

84

REDL: Don't snivel. You took *me* in.

COUNTESS: I didn't. I loved you . . .

REDL: Well, I didn't love you. I love Stefan. *We* just fooled one
another. Oh, I tried to hoax myself too, but not really
often. So: tonight's your wedding night. (*Pause.*) I tell you
this: you'll never know that body like I know it. The lines
beneath his eyes. Do you know how many there are, do
you know one has less than the other? And the scar behind
his ear, and the hairs in his nostrils, which has the most,
what colour they are in what light? The mole on where?
Where, Sophia? I know the place here, between the eyes,
the dark patches like slate—like blue when he's tired,
really tired, the place for a blow or a kiss or a bullet.
You'll never know like I know, you can't. The backs of his
knees, the pattern on the soles of his feet. Which trouble
him, and so I used to wash them and bathe them for
hours. His thick waist, and how long are his thighs,
compared to his calves, you've not looked at him, you
never will.

COUNTESS: Stop it!

(*Pause.*)

REDL: You don't know what to do with that. And now *you've*
got it.

COUNTESS: God, I'm weary of your self-righteousness and all
your superior railing and your glib cant about friendship
and the Army and the way you all roll out your little
parade: Michelangelo and Socrates, and Alexander and
Leonardo. God, you're like a guild of housewives pointing
out Catherine the Great.

REDL: So: you'll turn Stefan into another portly middle-aged
father with—what did you say once—snotty little longings
under their watch chains and glances at big, unruptured
bottoms.

COUNTESS: Alfred: every one of *you* ends up, as you well know,
with a bottom quite different, much plumper and far wider
than any ordinary man.

REDL: You think, people like you, you've got a formula for me.
You think I'm hobbled, as you say. But I'm free of you,

anyway. You, what about you, I can resist you!

COUNTESS: Do you know, remember, what you once said to me: I can never blame you. You are my heart.

REDL: I do blame you. I was lying. And Stefan is my heart. (*Pause.*)

COUNTESS: He said you told him I was Jewish. And what I looked like, what I *would* look like, drooping hairy skin and flab, and so on——

REDL: And now you're going to be a mother. You think you're a river or something, I suppose.

COUNTESS: That's right, Alfred. A sewer. Your old temple built over a sewer.

REDL: Sophia, why don't we . . .?

COUNTESS: No, Alfred. I'm in your grip. But I'll make no bargains. Do as you wish.

REDL: I bought him a beautiful new gelding last week.

COUNTESS: It should be back in your stables by now. And your groom's got all the other——

REDL: Get out.

COUNTESS: I'm going, Alfred. Do as you wish. You may think a trick was played on you once, but you've repaid and re-played it a thousand times over. I pity you: really——

REDL: Don't then. I'm really doing quite well.

(*She goes out.* KUPFER *comes in.*)

KUPFER: Well?

REDL: Well? Nothing . . . I suppose you think you're moving in?

KUPFER: Do you want me to draw up a full report on your file on the Countess?

REDL: That file is *my* property. And *you'll* do as you're told. I'm going to sleep. Close the shutters.

(KUPFER *does so.* REDL *falls asleep almost immediately on the bed. Soon little moaning noises are heard from him.* KUPFER *smokes a cigarette in the early evening light.*)

FADE

SCENE 2

The Red Lounge of the Sacher Hotel, Vienna. A string orchestra plays.
REDL *and* KUPFER *are drinking together.* KUPFER *is in a sour, watching mood.* REDL *is even cooler than usual and is smoking and appraising the other occupants of the lounge. He hails a* WAITER.

REDL: (*to* KUPFER). Another?

KUPFER: No. I'm going.

REDL: (*to the* WAITER). Just one then. So soon?
(*Pause.*)

KUPFER: Why St. Petersburg, for heaven's sake?

REDL: Because I've signed the order, and General Staff is not
    equipped to countermand orders. It works on the sweet
    Viennese roundabout method. Anyway, there's no one else.

KUPFER: But a whole year. I don't even speak Russian. It's
    nonsense.

REDL: Not to the Bureau. And now you *can* learn Russian, as I
    did. You should pick it up in half that time. It's the vowels
    that'll bring *you* down.

KUPFER: Thank you.

REDL: I'll get you back before the year's out. Don't worry.

KUPFER: You *are* sure of yourself, aren't you?

REDL: I have to be, don't I? And why not?
    (*He takes his drink from* WAITER.)
    No one is interested in doubts. This is an age of iron
    certainties, that's what they want to know about, run by
    money makers, large armies, munitions men, money
    makers for money makers. *You* were born with a silver
    sabre up your whatnot.
    (*Lifts his glass.*)
    St. Petersburg! I'll give you some names and addresses.

KUPFER: If only you'd at least admit it's because of Mischa.
    Why can't you be honest?

REDL: Because honesty is no use to you. People who don't want
    it are always yelling the place down for it like some
    grizzling kid. When they get it they're always
    miserable . . . Besides, Mischa is getting married, as you know.

87

KUPFER: I thought you'd put the stopper on that.

REDL: I didn't think we should tie him to a girl in a confectionery shop, a broad-faced, big-hipped little housefrau who can hardly read and write, and, what's more, doesn't care, all chocolates and childbirth. Still, if he wants that, he shall have it. It's a poor reward. Sad, too . . .

KUPFER: You do pick them, don't you?

REDL: Yes . . . But that is the nature of it. Marriage has never occurred to *you* for instance, has it?
(Pause.)
Since Stefan I've let them go their own ways. If that's all, if that's the sum of it, if that's what they want . . .

KUPFER: At least be honest with your*self*. The girl came round again last night.

REDL: Did she then? I told Max to throw her out. Next time he'll throw her down the stairs.

KUPFER: Then *she'll* end up in hospital as well.

REDL: Damn it, he's only got a nervous breakdown, or whatever they call it nowadays.

KUPFER: She says he's off his head.

REDL: Nonsense. He's always been over-strung. Maybe a bit unbalanced. He'll recover. And then he can marry her.

KUPFER: And he calls *me* cruel?

REDL: *You* were born like it. All your sort of people are. It's expected of you.

KUPFER: And what about *your* sort of people then?

REDL: Sometimes it's inescapable. I'm still nicer than you, Kupfer.

KUPFER: Why do you hate me, Alfred?
(Pause.)
Why then?

REDL: I've said often enough no one, and not you, is to call me Alfred in public . . . *(Hesitates.)*

KUPFER: Then why do you let me live with you?

REDL: You don't. I allow you a room in my apartment.

KUPFER: Exactly. You know, better than anyone, about jealousy.

REDL: It's a discipline, like Russian. You master it, or you
     don't. It's up to you, isn't it? Ah, here's Hötzendorf and
     Möhl.
KUPFER: Who's the boy?
REDL: Try and restrain your curiosity a little.
     (*They rise and greet* GENERAL HÖTZENDORF, GENERAL MÖHL
     and SUB-LIEUTENANT VIKTOR JERZABEK. *All salute stiffly,
     aware of their own presence in the lounge.*)
HÖTZENDORF: Ah, Colonel, the Lieutenant tells me that great
     automobile and chauffeur outside belong to you.
REDL: Yes, sir. New toy, I'm afraid.
HÖTZENDORF: Expensive toy. Don't see many like that.
     Thought it must belong to some fat Jew.
     (REDL *is discomfited.*)
     Oh, don't misunderstand me, the vehicle itself is in
     impeccable taste, Redl, like everything to do with you.
REDL: Will you join us, sir?
HÖTZENDORF: Just having a quick dinner. Brought some work
     with us, then back to the office.
MÖHL: The lieutenant is the only one who seems able to take
     down the General's notes fast enough.
HÖTZENDORF: Well, quickly then. I wanted a word with you.
REDL: Waiter! I was just celebrating some good fortune. My
     uncle in Galicia has just left me a legacy.
     (*Chairs are feverishly placed round the table for the arrivals.
     Everyone sits and orders.*)
HÖTZENDORF: Well done. Good. Yes, very good taste. Though
     I still prefer a good pair of horses, can't run an army with
     automobiles. No, but you know it's not that the Jews
     themselves are specially rotten. It's what they represent.
     For instance, no belief in service, and how can the Empire
     survive without the idea of service? Look at the Jews in
     Galicia, you must know, Redl, getting them into the
     army—quite impossible.
REDL: Indeed. *And* the high percentage of desertion.
MÖHL: Really? I didn't know that.
REDL: Nineteen per cent.
HÖTZENDORF: There you are. They're outsiders, they feel

outsiders, so their whole creed of life must be based on duplicity—by necessity.

REDL: I agree, sir. Even their religion seems to be little more than a series of rather pious fads.

HÖTZENDORF: Quite. We're all Germans, all of us, and that's the way of it. At least: Jews when they get on, remind us of it.

REDL: Which I suppose is a useful function.

HÖTZENDORF: Talking of that, Redl, I want to congratulate you on your handling of that Cracow spy affair. Everyone, absolutely everyone's most impressed and highly delighted, including the Emperor himself.

REDL: I'm deeply honoured, sir.

HÖTZENDORF: Well. You do honour to us. I see you already have the order of the Iron Crown Second Class. Möhl here is recommending you for the Military Service Medal.

REDL: I don't know what——

HÖTZENDORF: You know your stuff, Redl. You've an extraordinary understanding and intuition as far as the criminal intelligence is concerned. And, there it is, spies are criminals like any other. We all just use them like any thief or murderer.

MÖHL: That's right, he's right.

HÖTZENDORF: Cracow is our first bastion against Russia. If war breaks out, it's imperative those fortresses don't crack. They'll go for them first. If that little ring you rounded up had succeeded, we could have lost a war the day it started. From April I am proposing that you take over the Prague Bureau. Rumpler will direct Vienna.

REDL: I'm overwhelmed, sir.

MÖHL: To be confirmed of course.

REDL: Of course.

(HÖTZENDORF *raises his glass.*)

HÖTZENDORF: Congratulations, Colonel. To your continued success in Prague.

(*They drink the toast. The three arrivals rise at a signal.*)
Well, gentlemen. Goodbye, Redl. Oh, this young man tells me he's your nephew.

REDL: That's right, sir.

HÖTZENDORF: Good. Well, the General Staff can do with all the Redls there are around.

(*Salute. They pass through the lounge.* REDL *sits.* KUPFER *is dumbfounded.*)

REDL: Rumpler *would* stay in Vienna, naturally, with his coat of arms. Still, Prague . . .

KUPFER: Nephew!

REDL: Not yet. But I can't let an unknown Lieutenant from nowhere ride about Vienna in my new Austro-Daimler Phaeton. And I promised him faithfully the other day he could drive it himself sometime. He's quite clever mechanically.

(KUPFER *turns on his heel, and goes out.* REDL *lights a cigar and nods to the* HEAD WAITER.)

Send me the waiter over. I want the bill.

WAITER: Yes, sir.

REDL: No, not him. The young one.

FADE

SCENE 3

Hospital Ward. High, bare and chill. In an iron bed, sitting up, is a young man, MISCHA LIPSCHUTZ. *Beside him is a young girl,* MITZI HEIGEL. *The sound of boots striking smartly on the cold floor of a hospital corridor.* REDL *enters briskly. In greatcoat, gloves, carrying cane. An* ORDERLY *comes up to him respectfully.*

ORDERLY: Colonel, sir.

REDL: Colonel von Redl. To see Mischa Lipschutz.

ORDERLY: At once, Colonel, sir.

(*He leads him to* MISCHA's *bed.* MISCHA *hardly takes him in.* MITZI *looks up, then down again, as if she has become numbed by sitting in the same cold position so long.*)

ORDERLY: Shall I tell the young lady to go?

REDL: No. Mischa. How are you? I've brought you a hamper. (*No response. He hands it to the* ORDERLY.)
See that he gets all of it. Are you feeling any better? When do you think you'll be out then, eh? You look quite well, you know. . . . Perhaps you're still not rested enough. . . . Mischa . . . (*To* ORDERLY.) Can't he hear me? He looks all right.

ORDERLY: Perhaps your voice sounds strange, just a fraction sir? Mischa: Colonel Redl is here.

MISCHA: Mischa.

ORDERLY: How are you, the Colonel's asking?

MISCHA: I've been here quite a long time. I don't quite know how long, because we're absorbed into the air at night, and then, of course they can do anything they like with you at will. But that's why I keep rather quiet.

REDL: Who, Mischa?

MISCHA: They do it with rays, I believe, and atoms and they can send them from anywhere, right across the world, and fill you up with them and germs and all sorts of things.

REDL: Mischa, do you know where you are?

MISCHA: On a star, sir, on a star. Just like you. I expect you were sent to Vienna too, sir, because you are the same kind of element as me. The same dual body functioning.
(REDL *stands back. The* ORDERLY *shrugs, the* GIRL *doesn't look up.* REDL *walks out quickly.*)

FADE

SCENE 4

An hotel room near the Polish border in Galicia. It is cheap, filled with smoke but quite cosy. OBLENSKY *is sprawled on a low sofa, his tunic open, relaxed, hot with much vodka.* REDL *is slightly drunk too, though less cheerful.*

OBLENSKY: Come here, over here, have some more. Where are

you, Redl, you're always disappearing? Why are you so restless always? All the time limping home with scars, and now you've got a bitten lip, I see. Tell me now, about this new boy, what's it—Viktor——

REDL: He's not new.

OBLENSKY: I thought it was last February.

REDL: December.

OBLENSKY: Five months! Oh, I suppose that is a long time for you.

REDL: How often are you unfaithful to your wife?

OBLENSKY: When I'm not working too hard, and if I can arrange it, daily.

REDL: You seem to arrange most things.

OBLENSKY: Don't say it in that tone of voice. I was looking it up the other day. You've had eighty thousand kronen out of me over the years.

REDL: Out of Mother Russia.

OBLENSKY: Quite so. And she can ill afford your way of life.

REDL: She's had her money's worth.

OBLENSKY: Not over Cracow.

REDL: Oh, not again.

OBLENSKY: Well, later. Tell me about what's it, Viktor? Is he handsome?

REDL: Extremely.

OBLENSKY: Yes, but how handsome, in what way?

REDL: Tall, fair, eyes pale . . .

OBLENSKY: Is that what you like? Watery?

REDL: Tell me what *you* like.

OBLENSKY: My dear friend, ha!

(*He roars with laughter.*)

Nothing has the enduring, unremitting crudity of what I like. And *no* interest. I like nothing exotic. Now, the Countess, you know, Delyanoff, you used to write those strained love letters to, I could have had her at any time, naturally. But, nothing, no interest, here, whatsoever.

(*He crosses himself.*)

Too exotic. And I suppose intelligent. I can understand *you* trying her out very well. All I want is a lump, a rump, a

93

big, jolly roaring and boring, let us have no illusion, heaving lovely, wet and friendly, large and breasty lump! (*He roars, jumps up laughing, and fills their glasses.*) What I wouldn't do for one now! Yes, with you here too, Redl! Would that disgust you?

REDL: No.

OBLENSKY: Flicker of interest?

REDL: Very little I *have* watched.

OBLENSKY: Oh, dear. You make me feel cruder than ever. Tears of Christ! I'd make her jump and giggle and give her fun. All girls like fun. Even if they're educated. Do you give fun? Much?

REDL: Some, I imagine. Perhaps not too much. If I liked anyone it was because they were beautiful, to me, anyway.

OBLENSKY: Yes, I see. That's quite different. I don't see very much beauty. I mean I don't need it. You're a romantic. You lust after the indescribable, describe it, to yourself at least, and it becomes unspeakable.

REDL: You sound like a drunken Russian Oscar Wilde.

OBLENSKY: Me? Oscar Wilde!

(*He splutters with pleasure, and pours them out more vodka.*) Perhaps there's a cosy chambermaid here, if they have such a thing in this hole. I'll ask Stanitsin. Do you get afraid very often?

REDL: Yes.

OBLENSKY: (*switching*). I'll tell you some things that stick in my throat about you people. Do you mind?

REDL: If you wish.

OBLENSKY: Well, one: you all assume you're the only ones who can understand anything about yourselves.

REDL: (*politely*). Yes?

OBLENSKY: Well, two: frankly you go on about beauty and lyricize away about naked bodies as if we were all gods.

REDL: Some of us.

OBLENSKY: Or else you carry on like—rutting pigs.

(*They both address each other in a friendly way across the barrier they both recognize immediately.*) It isn't any fun having no clear idea of the future, is it?

And you can't re-make your past. And then when one of you writes a book about yourselves, you pretend it's something else, that it's about married people and not two men together . . . That is not honest, Alfred.

REDL: Don't be maudlin, Colonel.

OBLENSKY: Redl; you are one of those depressing people whom you always know you are bound to disappoint. And yet one tries. (*He looks quite jolly all the same.*) Well, you must be used to dancing at two weddings by this time. You've been doing it long enough.

REDL: You do enjoy despising me, don't you? Can we finish now?

OBLENSKY: Not till Cracow is settled. I don't despise you at all. Why should I? I don't care. I'm only curious.

REDL: My confessions are almost as entertaining as the Cracow fortifications.

OBLENSKY: You're quite wrong, quite, quite . . . I listen to you, I enjoy your company, see how much vodka we've drunk together, I don't drink with many people, Alfred. May I? I don't know anyone quite like you. It's taken a long time, hasn't it? You're giving nothing away this time.

REDL: What about Cracow?

OBLENSKY: Well, my dear friend, it was most embarrassing. Suddenly, my whole organization pounced on—*poum*! And who did it! You!

REDL: It was unavoidable. I felt there were suspicions . . .

OBLENSKY: But no warnings . . .

REDL: I tried, but it had to be.

OBLENSKY: Hauser was about my best agent.

REDL: I'm sorry. But you might have lost *me* otherwise.

OBLENSKY: Maybe. But if *I* don't turn up with something, something *now*, I'll be roasted. You've got to *give* me someone. And someone significant I can parade at a big trial, like your affair. Well?
(*Pause.*)

REDL: Very well. I have someone.

OBLENSKY: Who?

REDL: Kupfer.

OBLENSKY: Isn't he on your staff? St. Petersburg?

REDL: Yes.

OBLENSKY: Governments don't usually pounce on the diplomatic or military missions of other governments.

REDL: If it were outrageous enough.

OBLENSKY: Well, if you can fix it, and it's really scandalous.

REDL: I can.

OBLENSKY: Very well then, fix it, Redl.

(*He hurls his glass into the fireplace where it smashes.*)

Fix it. Now: We've hardly started yet.

FADE

SCENE 5

REDL's *apartment in Prague. A beautiful baroque room, dominated by a huge porcelain fireplace and double Central European windows.* VIKTOR *is in bed, naked from the waist up.* REDL *is staring out of the window angrily. Pause.*

VIKTOR: I think *I'll* get up. . . .

REDL: Why do you make such disgusting scenes with me? If you had the insight to imagine what you look like.

VIKTOR: Oh, don't. (*He flings his blond head across the pillow.*)

REDL: Oh, stop screaming, you stupid little queen! You don't want to get married, you whore, you urchin! You just want to bleed me to death. You want more. Dear God, if ever there was a ludicrous threat, you don't want the girl or any girl, you couldn't. I've seen her too, remember. *I* could, mark you, and *have*. But not you. When I think . . . How do you imagine you would ever have got a commission in a cavalry regiment, you, who would have bought you three full-blooded horses, and paid your groom and mess bills, *and* taught you to shoot like a gentleman, to behave properly as a Fire leader and be a damned piss-elegant

96

horseman in the field? You couldn't open your mouth and make an acceptable noise of any sort at all.

(VIKTOR *weeps softly*.)

You're so stupid you thought you could catch me with a shoddy ruse like that. You'll get no bills paid, nor your automobile, that's the bottom of it, you're so avaricious, you'll get nothing. You're so worthless you can't even recognise the shred of petty virtues in others, some of which I have still. Which is why you have nothing but contempt for anyone, like me, who admires you, or loves you, or wants and misses you and has to beg for you at least one day a fortnight. Yesterday, yesterday, I spent two excruciating hours at the most boring party at Möhl's I've ever been to, talking to endless people, couldn't see or hear, hoping you—God knows where you were—that you'd possibly, if I was lucky, might turn up. Just hoping you might look in, so I could light your cigarette, and watch you talking and even touch your hand briefly out of sight.

VIKTOR: I *do* love you.

REDL: In your way, yes. Like a squalling, ravenous, raging child. You want my style, my box at the opera instead of standing with the other officers. You're incapable of initiating anything yourself. If the world depended on the Viktors, on people like you, there would be no first moves made, no inexpedient overtures, no serving, no invention, no spontaneity, no stirring whatsoever in you that doesn't come from elsewhere . . . Dear Mother of God, you're like a woman!

(VIKTOR *howls*. REDL *pulls him out of bed by the leg and he falls heavily to the ground with a thump*.)

You've no memory, no grace, you keep nothing.

(REDL *bends over him*.)

You are thick, thick, a sponge, soaking up. No recall, no fear. You're a few blots . . . All you are is young. There's no soft fat up here in the shoulder and belly and buttocks yet. But it will. Nobody loves an old, squeezed, wrinkled pip of a boy who was gay once. Least of all people like me or yourself. You'll be a vulgar fake, someone even toothless housewives in the market place can bait.

(*Grabs his hair and drags him.*)

You little painted toy, you puppet, you poor duffer, you'll be, with your disease and paunch and silliness and curlers and dyed wispy hair and long legs and varicose veins like bunches of grapes and prostate and thick waist and rolling thighs and big bottom, that's where we all go.

(*Slaps his own.*)

In the bottom, that's where we all go and you can't mistake it. Everyone'll see it!

(*He pauses, exhausted. His dressing gown has flown open.* VIKTOR *is sobbing very softly and genuinely.* REDL *stands breathless, then takes the boy's head in his arms. He rocks him. And whispers*):

It's not true. Not true. You *are* beautiful . . . You always will be . . . There, baby, there . . . Baby . . . It won't last . . . All over, baby . . .

FADE

SCENE 6

Office of GENERAL VON MÖHL, TAUSSIG *is handing papers to the dazed* GENERAL.

TAUSSIG: This is the envelope, sir. As you see, it's addressed to Nicolai Strach, c/o General Postal Delivery, Vienna. It lay there for several weeks before it was opened by the Secret Police, who found it contained five thousand kronen and the names of two well-known espionage cut-outs, one in Dresden and another in Paris. The letter was re-sealed. Rumpler was informed immediately and we waited.

MÖHL: And?

TAUSSIG: Redl took three days' leave and motored in his automobile to Vienna where he picked up the letter. On Thursday evening.

(Pause.)

ÖHL: Redl?

(He might almost have burst into tears.)

AUSSIG: Sir. Then. His account at the Austro-Hungarian
Bank, unpaid bills for stabling, furniture, tailoring, *objets
d'art* and so on. Automobile maintenance, totalling some
fifty thousand crowns. Assets: a little over five, plus
valuable personal properties as yet unvalued. Some
securities worth perhaps eight thousand kronen. His
servant Max is owed a year's wages, but doesn't seem to
mind. A trunk full of photographs, women's clothes,
underwear, etc., love letters to various identified and
unidentified men, a signed oath from Lieutenant Jerzabek,
swearing not to marry during Redl's lifetime and only
afterwards by way of certain complicated financial losses in
Redl's will. Redl's will . . .

ÖHL: All right. General Von Hötzendorf must be informed at
once. No: I must do it. He'll go out of his mind. Redl!
How people will enjoy this, they'll enjoy this. The *élite*
caught out! Right at the centre of the Empire. You know
what they'll say, of course? About the *élite*.

AUSSIG: Perhaps it can be kept a secret, sir. Do you think? It's
still possible.

ÖHL: Yes. We must do it now. Where is Redl?

AUSSIG: The Hotel Klomser.

ÖHL: We'll see Hötzendorf, get his permission, and then we'll
go there, together, you and I. We'll need a legal officer,
Kunz I'd say. But he *must* be sworn to outright secrecy.
Those damned newspapers . . .

AUSSIG: Kunz is the man for that, sir.

ÖHL: Very well. Let's break the news to General Hötzendorf.

FADE

99

SCENE 7

REDL's *bedroom at the Hotel Klomser. Above his bed the black, double headed eagle of Austria and a portrait of Francis Joseph.* REDL *is seate at a bureau. In front of him stand* M.OHL, TAUSSIG *and* KUNZ. RED *signs a document, gives it to* KUNZ, *who examines it, then puts it into h briefcase which he straps up briskly.*

KUNZ: That's all, General Möhl . . .

REDL: You know, General, I know you'll be offended if I say
this because I know you're a deeply religious man, and
I . . . well, I've always felt there was a nasty, bad smell
about the Church. Worse than the Jews, certainly. As you
know, I'm a Catholic myself.. Who isn't? Born, I mean.
(*He takes the champagne bottle out of the bucket and pours a
glass.*)
Born. But I think I hate the Spaniards most of all. Perhap
that's the flaw . . . of my character . . . they *are* Catholics.
Those damned Spaniards were the worst marriage bargain
the Habsburgs ever made. Inventing bridal lace to line
coffins with. They really are the worst. They stink of
death, I mean. It's in their clothes and their armpits, quite
stained with it, and the worst is they're so proud of it,
insufferably. Like people with stinking breath always puff
and blow and bellow an inch away from your face. No, the
Spaniards are, you must admit, a musty lot, the entire
nation from top to bottom smells of old clothes in the
bottom of trunks.
(MÖHL *motions to* TAUSSIG, *who hands him a revolver.*
MÖHL *places it on the bureau in front of* REDL. *Pause.*)

TAUSSIG: Are you acquainted with the Browning pistol, Redl?

REDL: No. I am not.
(TAUSSIG *takes out the Browning Manual and hands it to* RED
Thank you, Taussig. Gentlemen . . .
(*They salute and go out.* REDL *pours another glass of
champagne and settles down to read the manual.*)

FADE

treet outside the Klomser Hotel. Early morning. MÖHL, TAUSSIG *and* NZ *wait in the cold.* REDL's *light is visible.*

JSSIG: (*looks at watch*). Five hours, General. Should we go up?

HL: No.

NZ: Forgive me, gentlemen. I'm going home. My wife is waiting for me. My work seems to be done.

HL: Of course.

NZ: Good night.
(*A shot rings out. They stare.* KUNZ *moves off.*)

HL: Well . . .
(*They light a cigarette.*)

FADE

SCENE 9

Chamber of Deputies. Vienna. Deputies. In the background blow- *of* The Times *for May 30th 1913, headed* 'SUICIDE OF AN *TRIAN OFFICER (FROM A CORRESPONDENT) VIENNA. MAY 29.'* *csimiles available from British Museum Newspaper Library.*)

UTY. The autopsy showed the bullet had penetrated the oral cavity, passing obliquely through the brain from left to right. Death must have been practically instantaneous due to haemorrhage. The question is, not who gave this officer the manual, but who allowed him to be given a revolver for this purpose at all?

ISTER: There will be no concealment of any irregularities.

UTY: Is it not true that this officer was exposed by reason of his official contacts with certain confidential elements in the military-political sphere for a period of some years, with

special duties in connection with the frontier protection a
the order of armament?

DEPUTY: Was not this same officer in the confidence of Von
Moltke the Chief of the Imperial German High Comman?

DEPUTY: Surely someone must have been around with the wit
or perception to have suspected something . . .

DEPUTY: Are we all asleep or what!
(*Roar.*)

DEPUTY: *What's become of us?*
(*Roars.*)

DEPUTY: Is it not true that he was, in fact, the son of one Mar
Stein, a Galician Jewess?
(*Uproar.*)
Why was this fact not taken note of?

MINISTER: The high treason which General Staff Colonel Red
was able to practise with impunity for a period of many
years is an occasion of the gravest possible public disquie
which is far from being allayed, if not actually increasing
This is due not only to the abominable crime committed
this officer—but more by the way in which the case has
been managed by the authorities of the Royal and Imperi
Army.

DEPUTY: Yes, but what do you *do* about it? What do you *do*?

MINISTER: We must not alarm the public more than is
necessary. It is true that the crime committed by Colonel
Redl against his country and the uniform he wore is felt
the most sensitive way by the whole population. Howeve
the only adequate protection of the honour of officers lie
in rigid standards, and if individuals act against the hono
of that class, the only helpful thing is the expulsion from
of those individuals by all the forms prescribed by law . .

FADE

SCENE 10

OBLENSKY's *office. Lights dimmed.* STANITSIN *working the magic lantern.*

OBLENSKY: Next!
    (*A photograph is snapped on to the screen.*)
STANITSIN: Schoepfer. Julius Gerhard. M.D., Ph.D., F.R.C.S., Member Institute Neuro Pathology, Vienna. Member Vienna Institute. Hon. Fellow of the Royal Society of London. Born Prague March 25th 1871. Family Jewish. Distinguished patients. List follows. Political and Military. In 1897, at the age of twenty-five he delivered a brilliant lecture on the origins of nervous diseases . . .

FADE

When *A Patriot for Me* was written it was not licensed for public performance by the Lord Chamberlain. A list of the cuts and alterations requested by the Lord Chamberlain—and to which Mr Osborne refused to agree—appears below.

Act I–1   'His spine cracked in between those thighs. Snapped. . . All the way up.'

I–4   This scene must not be played with the couple both in bed.

I–4   From: Stage direction—She moves over to the wall. . . .
To: . . . . Presently, he turns away and sits on the bed.

I–5   Reference to 'clap' and 'crabs'.

I–7   Reference to 'clap'.

I–10   Omit the whole of this scene.

II–1   Omit the whole of this scene.

III–1   The two men must not be in bed together.

III–1   From: 'You'll never know that body like I know it. . . .'
To? '. . . you've not looked at him, you never will.'

III–1   From: 'So: you'll turn Stefan . . .'
To: '. . . than any ordinary man.'

III–2   'You were born with a silver sabre up your what-not.'

III–4   'Tears of Christ!'

III–5   Omit the whole of this scene.

A Sense of Detachment

ACKNOWLEDGEMENTS

Acknowledgements are due as follows for permission to quote from copyright material:

For 'Change Partners' by Irving Berlin, Irving Berlin Ltd.: for 'In a Little Gypsy Tea-Room' by Joe Burke, Campbell, Connolly & Co. Ltd.: for 'Booze, Twentieth Century Booze' by Noël Coward; 'I'm on a See-Saw' by Vivian Ellis; 'Room 504' by George Posford; 'But Not for Me' by George Gershwin; and 'Ev'ry Time We Say Goodbye' by Cole Porter, Chappell & Co.: for 'Call Around Any Old Time', 'If You Were the Only Girl in the World', 'Goodnight', 'Yankee Doodle Boy' reproduced by permission of B. Feldman & Co. Ltd., 64 Dean Street, London W1V 6AU: for 'The Isle of Capri' by Wilhelm Grosz, Peter Maurice Music Co. Ltd.: for 'Goodbye', 'Five O'Clock Shadow', 'Meditation on the A30' and 'Ireland's Own' by John Betjeman, John Murray (Publishers) Ltd.: for 'Jean' by Rod McKuen, Twentieth Century Music Ltd.

CAST

CHAIRMAN

GRANDFATHER

OLDER LADY

FATHER

CHAP

GIRL

MAN IN STAGE BOX

SHIFTING PLANTED INTERRUPTER

SHIFTING PLANTED INTERRUPTER'S WIFE

STAGE MANAGER

The play was first performed at the Royal Court Theatre on December 4th, 1972. The cast was as follows:

CHAIRMAN	Nigel Hawthorne
CHAP	John Standing
GIRL	Denise Coffey
OLDER LADY	Rachel Kempson
FATHER	Hugh Hastings
GRANDFATHER	Ralph Michael
SHIFTING PLANTED INTERRUPTER	Terence Frisby
SHIFTING PLANTED INTERRUPTER'S WIFE	Jeni Barnett
MAN IN STAGE BOX	David Hill
STAGE MANAGER	Peter Jolley

Directed by Frank Dunlop
Designed by Nadine Baylis
Lighting by Rory Dempster

Act One

The curtain rises on a virtually empty stage except for a projection screen at the back, a barrel organ downstage and an upright piano. After a slight pause, the principal actors walk on carrying light bentwood chairs. The actors are the CHAIRMAN, a man in his mid-forties, the CHAP, who is slightly younger, the GIRL, who is younger still, the FATHER, who is about seventy, the GRANDFATHER, who is about ten years older and the OLDER LADY, who is about the same age. They place their chairs in position and look around them, at each other, the stage and all parts of the auditorium.

CHAIRMAN: Well, this looks like a pretty unpromising opening.

CHAP: Blimey, you're telling me. The Stage Management look more interesting than we do. Or that lot out there. (*Indicates audience.*)

CHAIRMAN: Oh, dear, what does one expect?

CHAP: Nothing, I suppose.

CHAIRMAN: True.

    (*The CHAP goes up to the projection screen.*)

CHAP: Oh, not one of *those*.

GIRL: I suppose you realize I haven't said anything yet?

CHAIRMAN: You will, you will.

CHAP: And paid for it.

GRANDFATHER: Overpaid, I expect.

CHAP: Right.

GIRL (*Points to barrel organ*): I hope no one's going to play that bloody thing. I can't stand barrel-organs.

CHAP: Oh, we'll have the bagpipes before we're finished, I expect.

GIRL: I can't stand the Scots either.

CHAP: I thought you were Scotch.

GIRL: Scots, you ignorant little bastard.

GRANDFATHER: Oh . . . is it going to be that sort of language?

GIRL: What sort of language?

CHAP: He means vaguely dirty, like we all use.

GRANDFATHER: I hope nobody's going to take all their bloody clothes off.

GIRL: Christ, so do I! All those limp, dangling dicks.

CHAP: And tits down to the knees.

OLDER LADY: Oh, I rather like all that.

GIRL: You would, you filthy old woman.

OLDER LADY: What did you say?

GIRL: You heard.

CHAP: Cloth ears. (*Points to* FATHER.) I hope this old sod isn't going to just sit there in his 1930's suit looking mysterious.

FATHER: I shall probably play the piano.

CHAP: You never played it very well.

GIRL: He's quite attractive.

CHAP: He's probably another 'exercise in nostalgia'.

GIRL: Oh, don't. Those boring T.V. chat shows!

CHAP: I shouldn't say that. You might find yourself on one.

GIRL: For what *they* pay?

CHAP: All you seem to do is talk about money.

GIRL: And why not? You don't think I get much from this bloody mean management, do you?

CHAP: Well, it's boring.

INTERRUPTER (*from stalls*): Hear, hear!

GIRL: Piss off!

GRANDFATHER: I may be old-fashioned . . .

GIRL: You are——

GRANDFATHER: But I still don't think young girls should talk like that.

CHAIRMAN: Not as old-fashioned as some of us.

INTERRUPTER: Dead right.

OLDER LADY: What did that man say?

GIRL: Some balls.

OLDER LADY: Who is he? Do we know him?

CHAP: Oh, I think he's *participating*, or something.

CHAIRMAN: No, just an obvious over-familiar theatrical device.

CHAP: Won't be the last one, either.

GRANDFATHER: Do you think we should offer him his money back?

GIRL: No, I don't!

CHAIRMAN: He's lucky to be here.

CHAP: *He* doesn't think so.

GIRL: He doesn't think anything just as long as he gets his salary at the end of the week. Can't wait for mine.

CHAP: Watch it. Or we may not be here tomorrow night at all.

GIRL: They've still got to give me two weeks' money.

CHAP: God, you are a Scot, aren't you?

CHAIRMAN: I don't think we should be nasty about the Scots. They'll think we've got it in for them, or something.

CHAP: Why not?

GIRL: Who cares?

CHAIRMAN: Exactly. Who cares?

GRANDFATHER: Good malt whisky.

GIRL: You're not going to burble on like that all the time, are you?

OLDER LADY: He's never been very interesting, I'm afraid.

CHAP: Ah, 'the theatre of antagonism'.

CHAIRMAN: The 'device of insult'.

GRANDFATHER: 'Oh, what a piece of work is Man . . .'

CHAP: Oh, belt up.

GIRL: I must say quoting Shakespeare is pretty cheap.

CHAIRMAN: Let's face it, it's all pretty cheap.

CHAP: *We're* pretty cheap.

GIRL: *I'm* not.

CHAP: Yes, we know about you. You're expensive.

GRANDFATHER: 'Oh, what a piece of work is Man . . .'

CHAP: Alas, poor old prick, I knew him well.

GRANDFATHER: How does it go on?

CHAP: 'A fellow of infinite jest, of most excellent fancy.' He has bored the arse off me a thousand times.

GIRL: Who?

CHAP (*in Shakespearean yokel type voice*): Why, he that is mad and sent into England!

GRANDFATHER: I suppose all life is a theatre.

CHAP: And all theatre is *laife*.

GIRL: What a profound insight!

CHAP: You mean *obvious*?

GIRL: Naturally.

INTERRUPTER: Is it all going to be as formless as this?

CHAIRMAN: Yes.

CHAP: I expect so.

GIRL: *You* try learning the bloody stuff. I've forgotten half of it already.

INTERRUPTER: You're trying to have it all ways, aren't you?

GIRL: As the actress said to the bishop.

INTERRUPTER: Do you think we can't see through this?

GRANDFATHER: I shouldn't think *he'll* sit through it.

GIRL: He will.

CHAP: We know, he's paid for it.

CHAIRMAN: Yes, I think we've had enough of him for a bit, don't you?

CHAP: Bit of your old Pirandello, like.

CHAIRMAN (*to* INTERRUPTER): Yes, I should go to the bar and have a drink.

GIRL: Don't think the Management will pay for it!

CHAP: I suppose *that's* a character trait, is it?

GIRL: What?

CHAIRMAN: Well, I suppose we'd better make some sort of start, though I don't know why.

GIRL: You either freeze to death or boil your knickers off.

INTERRUPTER (*walking out of auditorium*): Bloody right! Load of rubbish!

CHAP (*in pompous voice*): Hear, hear!

INTERRUPTER: My small boy could do better than this.

CHAP: Yes, I bet he likes small boys an' all.

NOTE: *If there are any genuine interruptions from members of the audience at any time, and it would be a pity if there were not, the actors must naturally be prepared to deal with such a situation, preferably the* CHAIRMAN, *the* CHAP *or the* GIRL.
These can be obvious, inventive or spontaneous, apart from the obvious responses like 'Piss off', 'Get knotted', 'Go and fuck yourself if you can get it up, which I doubt from the look of you', etc.

These could be adapted to the appearance or apparent background, like:

'Get back off to the shires, you married pouve,'

'If you're Irish, get out of the parlour.'

'And I hope the ship goes down in Galway Bay.'

'Get back to Golders Green, you hairy git.'

'Why aren't you in the West End, watching some old tatty expensive shit?'

Interrupter can return at any of these with any of the following abusive lines:

'What we want is family entertainment.'

'When you've had a hard day's work, you don't want to sit and listen to a lot of pseudo-intellectual filth.'

'Bourgeois crap.'

'Do you expect to get the young people into the theatre this way?'

'Who cares about them? What about us?'

'All too obvious, I'm afraid.'

'Like it doesn't do anything for me, man.'

'I hope that the women are being paid the same as the men.'

'Like what's it all for, man?'

'They did all this in the 1930's, only better.'

'I'm glad I haven't got any money in the show.'

And so on.

CHAIRMAN: Now where were we?

GIRL: Nowhere.

CHAP: Absobloodylutely nowhere.

(*From the loudspeakers comes the lush sound of the Adagietto from Mahler's* Fifth. *They all listen in silence for a while.*)

CHAIRMAN: Oh, I don't think we need *that*, do you?

CHAP: I don't know, I should think we probably do.

CHAIRMAN: Always used to sneer at it, I remember.

GIRL: Still do, some of them.

OLDER LADY: Rather good ballet music, don't you think?

CHAIRMAN: Oh Christ! (*to the* CHAP) Anyway, ask him to turn it down, will you?

FATHER: I can do a passable Melville Gideon.

GRANDFATHER: Now he really *was* good.

GIRL: Don't start yet.

CHAP: I like barrel organs.

CHAIRMAN: Yes, I know what you mean.

GIRL: Oh, do get on with it!

CHAP (*to* CHAIRMAN): Yes, you *are* the Chairman and she wants her pay packet.

GIRL: I'm just thinking about what I'm going to have to eat afterwards.

CHAIRMAN: Why should *I* be the Chairman?

CHAP: You know perfectly well.

GIRL: Yes.

CHAP: You're the best equipped academically, apart from which you're a brilliant promotionalist, an eyes upward grown-in Committee Man.

OLDER LADY: Very good actor too.

GIRL: What do you mean, good actor? He's a bloody amateur. Always has been. That's why people think he's so good.

CHAP: That's why he thinks he's so good too.

CHAIRMAN (*rising*): Well, if you're going to be like that . . .

CHAP: Of course we're going to be like that.

GIRL: Oh yes, don't be *faux naif*. Just get *on* with it.

CHAP: Oh, is that how you pronounce it?

GIRL: What?

CHAP: *Faux naif*, you avaricious little berk.

CHAIRMAN: *Right*, we'll start.

GIRL: Thank God for that. I'm hungry already.

CHAP: You would be.

CHAIRMAN (*addressing audience*): Er . . .

GIRL: Ladies and gentlemen!

CHAP: *That* lot?

CHAIRMAN: What else do I call them?

GIRL: Who cares?

CHAP: Perhaps some of them *are* ladies and gentlemen.

GIRL: I doubt it.

CHAIRMAN: Try not to be too censorious.

GIRL: I don't know what that means.

CHAP: Bitchy.

CHAIRMAN (*addressing audience again*): *Some* ladies and gentlemen and the rest . . .
(*There is an enormous commotion as the* MAN IN THE STAGE BOX *stumbles in noisily, looks around at the stage and leers drunkenly at the audience. He is wearing an enormous fake fur coat, a striped football scarf and cap*).

BOX MAN: What's all this then?

CHAIRMAN (*burying face in hands*): Oh no, not *that* old one!

CHAP: Yes, running short I'd say.

BOX MAN: Running short? *We've* been running short—all the brown ale we've had. Up Chelsea!

CHAP: And up you too!

GIRL: I never understand these gags. Exclusively male, I suppose.

CHAP (*in mock imitation of her*): Oh yes, I dare say that's *very* true. *Very* true. Exclusively male.

BOX MAN: What's *she* then? Women's Lib? (*Snorts at his own joke.*)

GIRL: I knew it was a mistake.

BOX MAN: It's a bloody mistake all right. Your mother's mistake!

GIRL (*to* CHAIRMAN): Such an amusing theatrical device.

BOX MAN: I'M IN THE WRONG BLEEDING THEATRE!

CHAIRMAN: We're all in the wrong bleeding theatre.

BOX MAN: Is this Drury Lane?

GIRL: No, and it's not *Fiddler on the Roof* either.

OLDER LADY: What did he say?

BOX MAN: *You* can drop 'em for a start!

OLDER LADY: I suppose you think I wouldn't?

BOX MAN: All right, don't bother. Is there a change of scenery?

CHAIRMAN: No, but I'm afraid there will probably be some music.

GIRL: If you can call a barrel organ music.

BOX MAN: Go on, Grandad, give us a tune!

GRANDFATHER: No respect left.

OLDER LADY: Why should they?

BOX MAN: I can't make head or tail of this lot.

GIRL: And you won't. No tits.

CHAP: Oh, he's not such a bad idea.

BOX MAN (*standing up and addressing the audience*): Well, if you're going to fuck the chicken, I'll dangle my balls in the pink blancmange.

GIRL: Now what's he talking about?

CHAP: Does it matter?

(*Enter from Dress Circle the* INTERRUPTER.

INTERRUPTER: Rubbish! I want my money back!

BOX MAN: Yes, well I'm going to go and have a slash.

GIRL: Yes, we know, after all that brown ale.

BOX MAN: Oh, I could do something for you, Daisy.

GIRL: My name's not Daisy and *you* couldn't.

(INTERRUPTER *disappears.*

GRANDFATHER *gets up slowly and plays the barrel organ gravely.*
The BOX MAN *joins in with the song and encourages the audience*
to join him.)

BOX MAN (*singing*):

> I don't care who you are
> Make yourself at home
> Put your feet on the mantel shelf
> Draw up a dolly and help yourself.

GRANDFATHER (*addressing* BOX MAN): Those are not the words.

BOX MAN: Well, you don't have to be like *that*! I've paid my
money, haven't I?

GIRL: No.

BOX MAN: Listen, you don't have to get all toffee-nosed with *me*.
Or any of these other good people. We *make* you, the likes
of you. Mr. John Public, that's what we are. Mr. and Mrs.
John Public.

GIRL: I hope you'll be very happy together.

BOX MAN: We are—what's wrong with that I'd like to know? It's
all right for you lot, sitting down there, looking all pleased
with yourselves, getting paid hundreds of pounds.

CHAP (*to* GIRL): There you are.

BOX MAN: Where would you *be*, I'd like to know——

GIRL: You're repeating yourself.

CHAP (*to* GIRL): So are you.

BOX MAN: Thank you, sir. Now you're a gentleman, I can see that.

GIRL: He can't even . . .

BOX MAN: That's enough of *your* lip. Don't think I wouldn't come
down there and smack your bottom—*and* enjoy it!

GIRL: I've no doubt, you poor old thing.

BOX MAN: All I said was he was civil and a gentleman.

GIRL: He's no more of a gentleman than you are.

CHAP: Good.

BOX MAN: Like some of these people here tonight. Look at them. Beautifully dressed, attractive women, lot of respectable people out there, including some of your real clever ones.

GIRL: Who do you think he's talking about?

CHAIRMAN: Yes, well I think we've had enough of *that*, too.

BOX MAN: What's that?

CHAIRMAN: I suggest, sir, that you come back later.

GIRL: Oh, *no*, please!

BOX MAN: I don't care what you say, I've paid my money and I'm going out for a slash.

CHAP: Perhaps it's not such a bad idea.

(BOX MAN *stumbles out of stage box with maximum of noise and so on*.)

CHAIRMAN: Shall I sit in the middle?

CHAP: Lucky Pedro, in the middle again.

GIRL: I suppose that's another joke?

CHAP: Masculine.

(BOX MAN *returns noisily. Shouts down at the actors*.)

BOX MAN: That's not funny, old man! Give yourself a kick in the pants!

CHAP: He pinched that from Peter Nichols.

CHAIRMAN: Actually, *he* pinched it from George Doonan.

BOX MAN: You're all a bloody lot of thieves and robbers! (*Staggers out*.)

CHAIRMAN: Well, as you seem to have suggested that my personality is best suited to imposing some order on this chaos——

CHAP: Or chaos on this order.

GIRL: As the case may be——

CHAIRMAN: I shall try to make a beginning.

INTERRUPTER (*from auditorium*): And about time, I say!

CHAIRMAN: Of sorts. Well, ladies and gentlemen and so on. The programme first, I suppose . . . Overpriced, as usual. Full of useless information. Like what part of Buckinghamshire the actors live in, how many children they've got, what their hobbies are and the various undistinguished television series that they've appeared in. On the front, there's the title.

GIRL: Awful.

CHAIRMAN: Yes, I'm afraid *that* will have to be changed.

CHAP: Too late now.

GIRL: Actually, 'Too Late Now' s not a bad title.

CHAP: It's too late all right.

GIRL: Wasn't there a song called 'Too Late Now'?

CHAP (*In T.V. Chat Show voice*): Ah yes, 'a rather predictable exercise in somewhat facile nostalgia'.

GIRL: Oh, do stop knocking everybody. Let him get on with it.

CHAP: You still won't get paid till Friday.

CHAIRMAN: As I was saying—what was I saying?

GIRL: The programme.

CHAIRMAN: Oh yes, well we've agreed that the title will have to be changed.

CHAP: The author's name is far too big.

CHAIRMAN: So is the director's, come to that.

CHAP: And who cares who *presented it*? What's that—just making a lot of 'phone calls, having long lunches and getting secretaries to do all the work.

GIRL: Don't talk to me about directors. If ever there was a bogus job, that's one all right.

CHAP: Just letting all the actors do the work, like finding where the doorknobs are, finding out what the play's about by getting up and doing it, while they tell you what a genius you are.

CHAIRMAN: I don't think that's entirely fair.

CHAP: Like doing Hamlet as a Pre-Raphaelite queen.

GRANDFATHER: I used to like the old musical comedies . . .

FATHER: And a good revue.

GIRL: Well, you ain't going to get it, either of you.

OLDER LADY: I quite like it when they take all their clothes off.

CHAIRMAN: I'm sorry, but shall I go on or not?

(BOX MAN *returns noisily*.)

BOX MAN: I suppose you went to Oxford and Cambridge.

CHAIRMAN: No, actually I was only at one of them. Oh, dear, I suppose one shouldn't be so rude.

BOX MAN: Toffee-nosed pouf! (*Goes out*.)

CHAIRMAN: I agree with you that I may be occasionally and unforgivably toffee-nosed, but I am not a pouf.

118

GIRL: Oh come off it—we all know about *you*.

CHAP: You either likes one thing or the other, that's what I always say.

BOX MAN: Hear, hear!

CHAIRMAN (*to* GIRL): If I may correct you, my dear—

GIRL: Oh now, he's *really* being the Chairman.

CHAIRMAN: Yes, as a matter of fact, I am, and I would point out to *you* that you are out of order.

BOX MAN: Hear, hear!

CHAIRMAN: You do not 'know all about me', as you put it, neither will you do so.

CHAP: I would like to support the Chairman on that.

GIRL: You would, but we'll have a right gusher of North Sea Gas out of you and your dreary life before this is over. I know that.

BOX MAN (*returning*): Do you want me to sort him out, Missus?

GIRL: No, just shut up.

CHAIRMAN (*to* BOX MAN): Did you have an enjoyable slash?

BOX MAN: Are you taking the mickey?

CHAIRMAN: No, I was asking what I thought was a friendly question.

BOX MAN: Well, I tell you, doesn't half pong in there!

CHAIRMAN: Yes, well I'm afraid we've been trying to put that right for years.

BOX MAN: When I think of what ordinary working-class people like me——

GIRL: You're not working-class, you're just a loud mouth.

CHAP: As well as pissed out of your arsehole.

GRANDFATHER: Oh dear, I wish you wouldn't.

OLDER LADY: I rather enjoy the freedom of expression of these young people.

GIRL: What do you mean young—he's middle-aged!

BOX MAN: When I think of what people like us, people like us who do a real job of work, not like you, *you've* never done a job of work . . .

GIRL: Piss off!

BOX MAN: . . . Pay for their seats with their hard-earned money, and don't you use that filthy language at *me*.

119

GIRL: Why not?

BOX MAN: Because you're an educated woman, and you ought to bleeding well know better.

GIRL: Well, I'm not educated and I don't know any better.

CHAIRMAN (to BOX MAN): I think you've made your point, sir.

BOX MAN: Sing us a song! Oh Christ, I've got to go back to that stinking hellhole again! (He blunders out.)

CHAP (sings):
'Oh God our help in ages past,
Our hope for years to come,
Our shelter from the stormy blast
(All join in)
And our eternal home.'

GIRL: Hymns!

CHAP: Sort of scraping the barrel.

CHAIRMAN: To get back to the agenda, if that's what you can call it—I think we have dealt or at least spent enough time on this dull programme, the cupidity of the author and director——

CHAP (at GIRL): And the actors.

CHAIRMAN: I will only add that as you will see, or have seen, or predicted, that this neither is nor was an entertainment——

CHAP (in American accent): Nor a significant contribution to the cultural life of Our Time.

GRANDFATHER: Try not to be too nasty about the Yankees.

CHAP: Very good to us during the war.

GIRL: Well, they won it, of course.

CHAP: Yes. Flooded us with food parcels and French letters.

GRANDFATHER: And after the war.

CHAP: That's right. Lease Lend.

GRANDFATHER: Easy to sneer.

CHAP: Quite right. At least they didn't have to 'Go In', like 'Going into Europe'.
(Stage lights flash out and either a still or film appears on the projection screen of Mr. Edward Heath, smiling and waving to the full blast of the last movement of Beethoven's Ninth.
They all watch in silence for a few moments, then the picture goes out and the music stops.)

INTERRUPTER: Cheap!

CHAIRMAN: I quite agree with you, sir.

INTERRUPTER: He's doing a good job!

CHAIRMAN: I quite agree with you about the cheapness aesthetically.
(BOX MAN *stumbles back*.)

BOX MAN: All right for him. What about the poor bloody workers!

GIRL (*to* CHAIRMAN): Can't you get rid of him? I thought you were supposed to have some sort of artistic responsibility or something.

BOX MAN (*shouting down at* GIRL): You know what *you* need, don't you?

GIRL: Don't tell me, I'll guess. Not that *you* could, anyway.

BOX MAN: I'll see you later.

GIRL: Not if I can help it.

BOX MAN: Here, where's the bar?

GIRL: Just leap over the edge of the box, and it's the first crawl to your left.

INTERRUPTER: I must say I quite agree! I could do with a good stiff one myself.

GIRL: It would be the first time.
(*Both the* BOX MAN *and the* INTERRUPTER *leave*.)

CHAIRMAN: No, it's not a device I really approve of.

GIRL: I wish you'd shut up saying 'device'.

CHAP: Give him a chance.

FATHER: I can do Turner Layton doing 'Transatlantic Lullaby'.

CHAP: Later. I'm afraid he's not very good at it.

GIRL: I thought he was supposed to be dead or something artsy-craftsy. (*to* CHAIRMAN) Well, isn't he?

CHAIRMAN: Oh God, why did I agree to do it?

GIRL: Because you like pretending you don't enjoy it.

CHAIRMAN: Right. *That's* the programme. *I* am the Chairman.

GIRL: Big deal.

CHAIRMAN: This girl is a—girl, I suppose. She will—er—do her best——

GIRL: For the money I'm getting?

CHAIRMAN: To stylize, or give some sort of life to, the various personalities—female, I mean—who thread their way through one man's particular experience.

GIRL (*to* CHAP): That should send them to sleep all right.

CHAP: Are they awake?

CHAIRMAN: Authentic, but not over-explicit, of a man's lifetime.

GRANDFATHER: Twentieth century.

CHAP (*sings*):

Booze, twentieth century booze, You're getting me down.

OLDER LADY: Well, of course, I was born in the nineteenth century.

FATHER: I was born in 1900. That's the same age as the century.

GIRL: How utterly fascinating.

CHAP: What the Chairman really means is this young lady——

GIRL: Thanks.

CHAP: Will come on with a few bitchy imitations of people she personally dislikes.

CHAIRMAN: *As* I was trying to say, I am the Chairman, he is some Chap, she is some Girl, that's his Father.

CHAP: Died 1940.

FATHER: Taught myself to play by ear so I'm not very good.

CHAP: Oh, I like the way you used to do 'There's an Old Fashioned House in an Old Fashioned Street'.

GIRL: I thought he was supposed to be dead.

CHAP: Like *you*.

(BOX MAN *returns*.)

BOX MAN: Come on then, let's put a bit of life into it then!

GIRL: *You* put a bit of life in it. You haven't done anything up till now.

CHAIRMAN (*pointing to* GRANDFATHER): And this gentleman is this chap's Grandfather. Except that he's alive still, and this Chap's Father's dead. (*Pointing to* OLDER LADY.) As for this lady, she appears to be quite attractive, but as for the rest, I am not sure. At least, not yet.

CHAP (*to* audience): So sort that out on your tambourines.

BOX MAN: Jolly good!

INTERRUPTER: I suppose we needn't ask if there's a *plot* or not!

CHAIRMAN: Quite correct, sir, you need not. However, I dare say we'll stick in some safe bit for the audiences, so that they can delude themselves that there is some intention and continuity.

GIRL: Either way they won't know.

CHAIRMAN: Of course.

BOX MAN: Sing us a song!

INTERRUPTER: Well, I'm going to complain to the Manager!

GIRL: Good. You *do* that.

INTERRUPTER: What's more, I shall go and see my M.P.

CHAP: Some south-east Tory, or right-wing Labour time-server.

BOX MAN: What about the old-aged pensioners?

CHAP: *You* should get an old prick's pension.

BOX MAN: They told me it was a musical.

CHAP (*sings*):
'I'm a Yankee Doodle Dandy . . .'

GIRL: There he goes again.

CHAP: 'A Yankee Doodle do or die . . .'
(*All join in.*)
'A real live nephew of my Uncle Sam,
Born on the fourth of July!'
(*During this, the Stars and Stripes flutter on the projection screen.*)

INTERRUPTER: Cheap!

BOX MAN: Mocking the poor bloody American flag now.

CHAP: We *can* mock the British one if you prefer.

CHAIRMAN: No, I don't think we do, do we?

INTERRUPTER: No, we don't.

BOX MAN: What about a SONG?
(*The stage lights dim, a frozen waste appears on the projection screen to the lone soprano sound from Vaughan Williams's* Symphonia Antarctica.)
I don't mean that sort of highbrow stuff.

INTERRUPTER: You don't call *that* highbrow, do you?

CHAIRMAN: No. Very middlebrow I'm afraid. (*to* CHAP) Ask the Stage Management, will you?
(*Projection and music stops.*)

CHAIRMAN: Right, let's sing him a song then.
(*They all line up and sing the following to the tune of* Widdicombe Fair

ALL:
Harold Pinter, Harold Pinter,
Lend me your grey mare,
All along, down along, out along lea,
For I want to go to
Printing House Square,

With Arnold Wesker,
David Storey,
Edward Albee,
Must get in an American,
Charles Wood,
Charlie Farnsbarns,
Christopher Hampton,
Sammy Beckett,
Sammy Someone,
Edna O'Brien,
Because she's a Woman,
And we're in enough trouble already,
Old Uncle Sammy Beckett and all,
And old Sammy Beckett and all.
(*Repeat verse to a dance.*)

CHAP: Well, now *I'm* going for a slash.

CHAIRMAN: And *I'm* going for a drink.

OLDER LADY: Is this the interval?

GIRL: The interval? You must be joking!

GRANDFATHER: Oh, can we go now?

CHAIRMAN: Everyone's free to do as they wish.
(*On the projection screen, there is a picture of the Trooping of the Colour. The men all stand up. Very brief, this.*)

CHAIRMAN (*to the* audience): That wasn't actually meant to be disrespectful.

BOX MAN: Ha ha di bloody ha ha! Where's the bar?

GIRL: By the men's loo, you drunken oaf.

INTERRUPTER: Take it off!

CAST (*to* INTERRUPTER): You take yourself off.
(*They all turn and dance off to the tune of* The Laughing Samba. *As the auditorium lights come up, the* CHAIRMAN *returns and starts to turn the handle of the barrel organ which plays* Roll out the Barrel. *He then signals to the prompt corner. A* STAGE MANAGER *appears to take over the handle, the* CHAIRMAN *looks at his watch and saunters off. After a few moments, the* STAGE MANGER, *clearly bored by the barrel organ, stops turning it, and goes off as well.*)

Act Two

As the audience returns, if indeed it does return, the house lights are up and an extremely loud Pop Group is blaring out over the loudspeakers, against the Pop Group's still photograph on the projection screen. On stage, the STAGE MANAGEMENT *and* STAGE HANDS *and so on are dancing, some in an off-hand and some in a rather demented manner. After a while, and the* STAGE MANAGER *will have to decide on this, when what is left of the house has got back in, some of them will look at their watches and start to wander off the stage.*

The BOX MAN *does his usual entrance, clutching a crate of brown ale, one bottle of which he is tippling. He smiles cheerily round at the audience, standing up and waving at them.*

BOX MAN: This sounds a bit more like it! I came here to be
   entertained, I don't know about you.
INTERRUPTER (*settling into his seat*): So did I. Doesn't seem very
   likely *now*. That Box Office Manager was quite insulting.
BOX MAN: Dead right, sonny boy! So he was to me. Right
   gaffer's man you've got in there. Boss's man. (*Shouting at
   the stage.*) Well, get on with it! (*Down to the* INTERRUPTER.)
   I complained about the toilet.
INTERRUPTER: Good . . . I've got a tube to catch.
BOX MAN: Never you mind, sonny boy. If it doesn't buck up a
   bit, we'll all have a few jars and a general piss up.
   (*He smiles broadly around him*) O.K.? (*He starts to sing.*)
   Why are we waiting,
   Why are we waiting . . .
INTERRUPTER (*joining in*):
   Why are we waiting,
   Oh why, oh why . . .

(STAGE MANAGER *appears*.)

STAGE MANAGER: That won't get you very far, you know.

BOX MAN: It won't get *you* any bloody far either, if you're not careful. Just get on with it. They burn down places like this, you know.

INTERRUPTER: Oh, I don't believe in violence. But I don't see why one should sit and be insulted. Quiet protest is quite sufficient.

STAGE MANAGER: All right. Start Dim.

(*He goes off, and the house lights do indeed start to dim as the* FATHER *enters and sits down at the piano. He starts playing and sings a snatch of* On The Isle Of Capri. *He then sings* In A Little Gypsy Tea-Room *as his son, the* CHAP, *enters. They sing together*.)

FATHER AND CHAP:

    'In a little gypsy tea-room,
    You stole my heart away,
    It was in a little gypsy tea-room,
    I fell in love one day . . .'
    (GIRL *enters*.)

GIRL: And he's such a thumping cad . . .

    (*The* CHAP *sings to his* FATHER'S *accompaniment, addressing himself to the* GIRL.)

CHAP:

    'I am only a strolling vagabond,
    So good night, pretty maiden, good night,
    I am off to the hills and the valleys beyond,
    Good night. . .'

INTERRUPTER: Joan Littlewood did this years ago.

CHAP: 'Good night . . .'

GIRL (*to* INTERRUPTER): Piss off.

BOX MAN: Yes, give the boy a chance.

CHAP:

    'So good night, pretty maiden, good night.
    I come from the hills,
    And the valleys beyond,
    So good night, pretty maiden, good night.'

GIRL: All right. That'll do. (*to* BOX MAN) *He's* no boy.

BOX MAN: I want to see Val Doonican.

CHAP: And the Black and White Minstrels.

GIRL: Oh, he'll black up for you if you like.

INTERRUPTER: I like something entertaining, but that leaves you with something to think about afterwards.

GIRL: Well, forget it.

(*During this exchange,* CHAIRMAN *enters and starts to sing, again to the* FATHER'S *accompaniment.*)

CHAIRMAN: 'Oh, my love is like a red, red rose . . .'

(*to audience*) Join in all you old folks—we still need your money while you're here—

GIRL: Oh, my God! *His* love!

CHAIRMAN: 'That's newly sprung in June . . .'

(*to audience*) And all you youngsters too, even if you can't remember the words. You'll be with us a bit longer if you're lucky.

BOX MAN: We don't want any of that modern rubbish.

GRANDFATHER: 'Everyone suddenly burst out singing . . .'

CHAIRMAN:

'Oh, my love is like the melody
That's sweetly played in tune . . .'.

(*to* GIRL): I do hope you're not going to be cheap and obvious about the Scots.

GIRL: I couldn't be bothered, actually.

(*She immediately dances to a number by the* Supremes *with the* CHAP. *This lasts as long as it will seem to hold.*)

(*to* CHAP): You're not very good, are you?

CHAP: No . . .

(*Once again, while this has been going on, the* GRANDFATHER *has entered and sat down on his chair.*

There is a silence, or if there isn't a silence, the actors will have to improvise. However, when the next stage is reached, GRANDFATHER *rises slowly and also sings.*)

GRANDFATHER:

'Rock of ages cleft for me,
Let me hide myself in thee,' (*etc.*)

CHAP: Very good.

GIRL: Of course he's good.

INTERRUPTER: 'Ancient and Modern' now, is it?

BOX MAN: Sounds *bloody* ancient to me. Who wants a brown ale?

CHAIRMAN (*to* BOX MAN): I shouldn't overplay it too much.

BOX MAN: Don't you get grotty with me! She's dead right.

> (*Pointing at the* GIRL): You're just a moaning old posh-voiced pouf.

> (OLDER LADY *enters.*)

> Come on, darling, sing us a song, or show us your knickers.

OLDER LADY: I will if you like.

CHAIRMAN (*to* OLDER LADY): What *are* you going to do?

FATHER: *I* know.

> (*He starts to sing as he plays the piano a fair pastiche of Jack Buchanan.*)
>
> 'Good night, Vienna,
> You golden city of a thousand dreams . . .'
>
> (*As he plays and sings, the* OLDER LADY *and the* GRANDFATHER *execute a very dashing tango together. The* BOX MAN *applauds at the end of it.*)

INTERRUPTER: God, how sentimental!

BOX MAN: Give the old bag a break, or I'll come down and give you a right duffing up.

OLDER LADY (*to* BOX MAN): Thank you very much.

> (*The* FATHER *does his introduction to* If You were The Only Girl In The World *and* OLDER LADY *sings to the audience.*)
>
> 'If I were the only girl in the world,'

GRANDFATHER (*rising*):

> 'And I was the only boy,'

CHAP (*also rising and singing*):

> 'Nothing else would matter in the world today,'

GIRL (*rising and singing and taking the* CHAP'S *hand*):

> 'We would go on loving in the same old way.'

OLDER LADY, GRANDFATHER, CHAP AND GIRL (*all join hands and sing the rest of the chorus*):

> . . .'If you were the only girl in the world
> And I was the only boy.'

INTERRUPTER: Oh God, I can't stand any more of this.

BOX MAN: Bloody good.

> (*The* CHAIRMAN *lifts his eyes to heaven or at least somewhere above his usual line of vision and addresses the* INTERRUPTER.)

CHAIRMAN: I think I really do have to agree with you this time.

INTERRUPTER: And so you should. (*He gets up and goes out.*)

BOX MAN: Piss off!

GIRL (*to* BOX MAN): Thank you, sir, she said.

BOX MAN: You know what *you* need.

GIRL: Yes, you told us all that before.

CHAIRMAN: Does anyone remember where we were?

GIRL: You must be mad.

(*The* BOX MAN *rises and sings.*)

BOX MAN:

'Oh, he's football crazy,

He's football mad,

Since he joined the local football club . . .'

CHAIRMAN: I know—'He's lost the wee bit of sense he had.'

GIRL: If I were a man, my balls would hurt.

CHAP: Well, thank God you're not.

CHAIRMAN: Anyway, it's 'footba' crazy', not 'foot*ball*'. Anyone can see *you're* not a Scot.

BOX MAN: Show us your kilt! What's your tartan, then? The Macpouves I suppose.

CHAIRMAN (*wearily*): I had an idea you were going to say that.

GIRL: We *all* had an idea he was going to say that.

CHAIRMAN: Yes, now this Chap was going to tell us about his life.

GIRL: That's what we're all afraid of.

CHAIRMAN: So, old um—

GIRL: Chap.

CHAIRMAN: I think the floor is what they call 'yours'.

BOX MAN: Give him a big hand! He's only just started. You never know. You might see him on the telly one day.

GIRL: Best place for him.

CHAIRMAN: Hear, hear.

(*The* CHAP *goes over to his* FATHER *at the piano and puts his arm round his shoulders.*)

CHAP: You needn't sit there all the time, you know.

FATHER: No, it's all right, I quite like sitting here.

GIRL: You've already said he's dead anyway.

GRANDFATHER: Missed the twentieth century. I didn't . . .

OLDER LADY: No, neither did I. I'm rather glad, aren't you?

CHAP: No.

BOX MAN: We shouldn't have missed *you*.

(*The* INTERRUPTER *appears from another part of the house.*)

INTERRUPTER: Yes, I'd like to know what you'd have done without decent dentists and anaesthetics. Can't see you biting on to a leather belt.

CHAP: Nor you, either.

BOX MAN: Let him say his piece. It's a free country.

CHAIRMAN: It's not a free country.

BOX MAN: It's not a free country.

CHAP: As I was about to say——

(*The* GIRL *goes into another* Supremes *type dance, the* CHAP *joins her. The music finishes suddenly.*)

CHAP (*to* GIRL): Finished?

GIRL. Yes. Do carry on.

CHAP: As I was saying——

BOX MAN: What was he saying? This brown ale they sold me in the bar tastes like old horse piss.

GIRL: How would you know?

CHAP: . . . I was born——

GIRL: That's a promising start.

CHAP: And original too.

CHAIRMAN: Oh, do stop it, the two of you. (*to the* CHAP) Do you think you could get on with it?

INTERRUPTER: What do you mean 'get on with it'? He hasn't started yet.

BOX MAN: Give the boy a chance.

(*The* CHAP *advances downstage and taking his time, he surveys the audience and addresses them.—If there is still any left.*)

CHAP:

The last time that I saw the King,
He did the most curious thing,
With a nonchalant flick,
He pulled out his dick,
And said: 'If I *play*, will you *sing*?'

INTERRUPTER: Filth!

GIRL: Just bloody boring.

OX MAN: I was in my cradle when I heard that one.

IRL: Cradles weren't invented when *you* were born.

HAP: I am going to make a sort of shortish speech about my life and women.

IRL: Wouldn't you guess?

OX MAN: Why, I've had more——

HAP: Yes, than hot dinners. Except my dinners were probably a bit hotter and slightly more interesting.

OX MAN: I'll come down and sort you out too!

HAP: No, you won't.

CHAIRMAN: Yes, he's quite right. You're just an underpaid——

IRL: Overworked——

CHAIRMAN: Exactly. What was it?

IRL: 'Device' is what you keep saying.

HAP: Now the first girl I really remember lusting after——

IRL: Wake me up when he's finished.

HAP: Was actually a woman.

(*They all change places and take up* T.V. *Chat Show poses.*)

I don't know *what* age she was really. She could have been twenty-one or thirty-one. All I remember is that she had a small boy called Malcolm about three years old, I should imagine, and a bit younger than me.

(*The* CHAIRMAN *clears his throat and becomes the* INTERVIEWER *to all the others.*)

CHAIRMAN: Now, J. Waddington Smith, you've just come from this play tonight—Did you think it came off at all? Or would you call it a total disaster?

GRANDFATHER: Not a total disaster, no. On the other hand——

IRL: On the other hand——

GRANDFATHER: I must confess it did have *some* enjoyable moments.

HAP: Oh, say that would you?

ELDER LADY: I quite enjoyed it. But then I suppose I'm easily pleased.

IRL: Oh no, you're not. You're the worst audience in the world.

HAP: Usual easy obligatory cracks about critics.

ELDER LADY: Well, naturally.

IRL (*fiddling with her hair*): But he really has got a bit too

131

predictable now, hasn't he? (*to* CHAIRMAN): They are getting me fiddling with my hair in the intellectual winsome bit, aren't they?

CHAIRMAN: Yes, but I shouldn't worry about it too much. I've already told them that——

GIRL: Device——

CHAIRMAN: Up in the Box not to overdo it too much.

OLDER LADY: Quite right.

CHAIRMAN (*to the* CHAP): It struck me that there was a certain amount of strident waffle. What would you say to that?

CHAP: Oh, I agree. After all, there ought to be a bit more to it than that?

GIRL: Oughtn't there?

CHAIRMAN: I agree. Didn't there? What did you think about the devices?

CHAP: The theatrical ones, you mean?

GIRL: Well, we did go to the *theatre*, didn't we?

FATHER: What *is* all this?

CHAP: They call it television.

GIRL: Yes, you really died before all that.

CHAP: Lucky old bugger.

CHAIRMAN: We're having a 'lively intellectual confrontation'.

CHAP: 'Making the news'.

CHAIRMAN: Do you mind? 'The first with the news'. (*Rising*) I think we've *done* this for the moment, anyway, don't you?

CHAP: Oh, yes.

(*They all change around seats with the* CHAP *now in the middle* Oh, yes . . . The lady with the three year old boy.

GIRL: Malcolm.

INTERRUPTER: Why don't you give the *young* people a chance?

CHAP: Why don't you give *us* a chance?

BOX MAN: You take a chance, darling.

GIRL: Don't be disgusting.

CHAIRMAN: Why shouldn't he be? He's paid his money. As he say

GIRL: I doubt it.

BOX MAN: And I want it back!

INTERRUPTER: So do I.

(*All sing the Stoke City football song* We'll Be With You,

which also plays over the loud speakers, led by the BOX MAN, *who twirls his scarf, etc., bawling, while some of the cast stand up to the Wembley type stadium sound.)*

AP: Well, to continue if that's possible——

AIRMAN: If anything's possible . . .

AP: There were the twins. One was called Gloria, I know. And I think the other was Pat. But Pat was the nice one, Gloria was the dirty one.

RL: Oh, yes.

AP: Then there was a younger, blonde fat one, but I don't remember her name. But I do think she was more sort of humiliating than the rest. Then there was my Auntie Viv. She had very dark, curly hair.

THER: I used to call her the Gypsy Queen.

AP: That's right. But she had a funny way with handling the children. And I remember she said to me, 'Don't lift your trousers'—we used to wear what were called 'short trousers' then—'when you go to the toilet'.

RL: Are you going to go on much longer?

AP: Then there was Arabella.

L: Arabella!

AP: Yes. She was twenty-one and I was about ten.

L: And you 'would have died for her'.

AP: Yes, I would have died for her. She had a young man, who was an old man of twenty-eight. And we all three of us used to go for walks on the Downs. In the fog with the destroyers wailing and the invisible convoys.

L: How romantic.

AP: Not at all. He (*pointing to* FATHER) was dying of T.B.

ANDFATHER: Oh well, they used to die of it then.

AP: Like *flies*, in my family. My sister went and my God, did I resent it. What she left *me* lumbered with.

L: Next.

P: Next? Oh yes. Then there was Betty. She was a Brown Owl. And then a strapping great Girl Guide. Christ, I was mad about *her*. I used to follow her down the streets from school—it was a state school I suppose you'd call it—and pretend I wasn't.

GIRL: What did she look like?

CHAP: Can't quite remember. But very dark blue eyes and hair—thick. Showed her legs off a lot but not too much.

GIRL: Very sensible. Next.

CHAP: There was somebody, I think she was called Audrey. She was a frightful bully and had a gang of boys mostly and used to sit on your head and try to suffocate you. Red hair, I think.

GIRL: Ginger minge in your nostrils. That must have been nice.

CHAP: Then there was Gladys.

GRANDFATHER: I used to know a Gladys.

GIRL: Who doesn't? What about her?

CHAP: Nothing much, really. She just said one day she'd only ever really liked me because I had wavy hair.

GIRL: How awful.

CHAP: I suppose it was fashionable at the time.

GIRL: Why does it have to *be about* anything?

CHAIRMAN: The Second World War . . .

GIRL: Vietnam . . .

CHAIRMAN: 'Luxuriantly bleak' I would say, wouldn't you?

CHAP: Yes, but 'martially lyrical'.

GIRL: Images! Who wants them? You can have them any old time.

OLDER LADY: I suppose it's all really just about things like music and fucking.

CHAIRMAN: Yes, but I suppose we've got to *discuss* it.

GIRL (*to* CHAP): Yes?

CHAP: I don't think I can.

GIRL: Oh, don't start blubbing, it's too early.

CHAIRMAN: Much too early.

CHAP: I can't go through the *whole* list.

GIRL: We're not asking you to. Next.

CHAP: Then there was Shirley and her sister.

GIRL: What about them?

CHAP: I just wonder what happened to them, that's all.

GIRL: Well, we all wonder that sort of thing.

CHAP: Shut up, you lousy bitch. I wouldn't tell you anyway.

GIRL: And then?

134

CHAP: Well, believe it or not, there was Fanny.

BOX MAN: Annie and Fanny!

CHAP: That's right. The Fan Dancer who fell down on her Fan.

BOX MAN: Do you know the one about the crocodile shoes?

GIRL: Yes.

OLDER LADY: Oh yes, *I've* heard that one. It's awfully good.

BOX MAN: Are you bloody sure you've heard it?

CHAIRMAN: Yes.

BOX MAN: I'll bet you don't know what it's——

CHAP: Yes. It's got *three* punch lines.

CHAIRMAN: Next.

CHAP: Then there was Rosemary.

GIRL (*to the* INTERRUPTER): There's Rosemary for *you*.

INTERRUPTER: We don't know who any of these people *are*. What they're *doing*. Where it's taking *place*. Or anything!

OLDER LADY: Give the boy a chance.

CHAP: What? Oh, Rosemary.

GIRL: Yes, Rosemary.

CHAP: Ah yes, well, she had the rags up all the time.

GRANDFATHER: Well, they can't help it, you know.

CHAIRMAN: Well, he's got a point there.

CHAP: No, but she had it all the bloody time. I mean like all over the graveyard in Norwich Cathedral.

GIRL: Norwich—you mean like——

CHAIRMAN Yes. (*wearily*) Knickers off ready when I come home.

CHAP: I mean, Women's *Insides*. I've been walled up in them and their despairs and agony ever since I can remember.

GIRL: Perhaps you should try it yourself.

CHAP: I'm not strong enough.

GIRL: No, you're not.

INTERRUPTER: I think this sort of talk is highly embarrassing. My own wife is in the audience and I may say that she is undergoing what I can only call to someone like you, an extremely difficult——

GIRL: Period——

INTERRUPTER: No. I would say more than that. Expected but dramatic experience in her life.

GIRL: You mean she's got the Hot Flushes?

CHAP: Well, let me tell you, mate, *I've* had them for forty years.

GIRL: And you look it . . . So we've got to Rosemary.

CHAIRMAN: Yes.

CHAP: Oh, I don't remember them. Then there was Jean, I suppose.

GIRL (*dances and sings*): 'Jean, Jean . . .'

BOX MAN: You'll get no awards for *this* lot.

CHAP: She was really good and big and well-stacked and knew how to——

GIRL: Get you on the job.

CHAP: Christ, I was only nineteen! I could do it *nine times* in the morning.

CHAIRMAN: Nine times. Could you really?

GIRL: There's not much impressive in that.

CHAP (*in bad Scots accent*): 'Oh, there's not much impressive in that'. We've all had *colds*.

GIRL: And then there are all those dreary wives of yours.

CHAP: That's right. Those dreary wives of mine . . . They all think I'm a pouve.

GIRL: I'm not surprised.

OLDER LADY: I don't think she should have said that to him.

GRANDFATHER: I don't know what they are talking about. *Any* of them.

CHAP: The first one was pretty good in the sack.

GIRL: So you keep telling us. She looks pretty awful *now*.

CHAP: My fault.

CHAIRMAN: I don't think I'm being compromising but——

GIRL: But——

CHAIRMAN: Well, I do feel, and I know you're going to yawn or laugh——

BOX MAN: Sing us a song!

CHAIRMAN: We will, my friend, I'm afraid we certainly will.

CHAP: Oh yes.

CHAIRMAN: But there are certain dark, painful places we shouldn't expose—for our own sakes and those of others.

CHAP: Actresses are pretty rotten lays.

GIRL: So are actors.

OLDER LADY: I've just been reading some material that's been sent to me.

136

GIRL: What's *she* on about?

OLDER LADY: They seem to call it pornographic. But it looks quite interesting to me.

GIRL: So it would, you dirty old bitch.

BOX MAN: I watch T.V. most nights of the week and all I can say is that the general standard of programmes is deplorable.

CHAP: Say that again.

BOX MAN: Deplorable.

CHAP: That's better.

OLDER LADY (*reading from brochure*): 'This month we've got "The Virgin Bride was to be Raped".' How *fascinating*. 'This is the lead novelette. Then after "The Letters to Lucille"——'

GIRL: Who's Lucille?

OLDER LADY: I don't quite know. It doesn't say. But it goes on: 'We have a picture story about what a released convict is going to do to the first woman he sees when he gets out.'

BOX MAN: Come on, let's have a bit of *that*, then.

OLDER LADY: 'Next comes Part Two of "Sex in a Scout Camp". After that, Part Two of a novelette called "Young Orgy".'

BOX MAN: Get in there, it's your birthday.

CHAIRMAN (*despairingly*): We really do have to get rid of him, don't we? I mean we *are* all *agreed*?

INTERRUPTER: Get rid of the lot of you, *I* say.

OLDER LADY (*reading*): 'Then we finish with a girl masturbating herself in both her holes at one time.'

BOX MAN: Brown ale, anybody?

(*The lights dim and on the projection screen appears a column of marching British sailors. In the meantime, on the loudspeaker, the Band of the Royal Marines plays* A Life on the Ocean Waves, *naturally, at full blast. The* BOX MAN *joins in. When this has finished, the* CHAIRMAN *speaks, as do the others, and the same ritual is repeated more or less after each piece of so-called pornography is gravely but interestedly intoned by the* OLDER LADY.)

CHAIRMAN:

'Oh wad some Pow'r the gifte gie us,
To see oursels as others see us!

It wad frae mony a blunder free us,
And foolish notion.'

CHAP:

'Oh England, full of sin, but most of sloth;
Spit out thy phlegm, and fill thy breast with glory.'

GIRL:

'Love is a circle that doth restless move
In the same sweet eternity of love.'

CHAP (*at* GIRL):

'I do love, I know not what;
Sometimes this, and sometimes that.'

GRANDFATHER:

'Some days before death
When food's tasting sour on my tongue,
Cigarettes long abandoned,
Disgusting now even champagne;
When I'm sweating a lot
From the strain on a last bit of lung
And lust has gone out
Leaving only the things of the brain;
More worthless than ever
Will seem all the songs I have sung,
More harmless the prods of the prigs,
Remoter the pain,
More futile the Lord Civil Servant——'

CHAIRMAN: I think that perhaps at this stage we should say something else.

INTERRUPTER: You're telling us!

CHAIRMAN: Yes, well, you *may* have your chance later, my friend.
'I see phantoms of hatred and of the Heart's
Fullness and of the Coming Emptiness.'
(*The* CHAIRMAN *comes downstage and addresses everyone*):
Yes, just wait a moment.
'I turn away and shut the door, and on the stair
Wonder how many times I could have proved my worth
In something that all others understand or share;
But oh! ambitious heart, had such a proof drawn forth
A company of friends, a conscience set at ease,

138

It had but made us pine the more. The abstract joy,
The half-read wisdom of demonic images,
Suffice the ageing man as once the growing boy.'

BOX MAN: We don't wish——

CHAIRMAN: No, my friend, and you may well be right. But we
are all plagiarists, as even you. As Brecht said once and
Shakespeare better than us all.

GIRL: He's getting quite good, isn't he?

OLDER LADY (*reading again*): ' "Waterloo Bridge". The classic story
as in the film of a young girl met and seduced by an officer
during the Blitz of London. She gets fucked in a bomb
shelter while sitting beside some people that take no
notice——'

CHAP: Take no notice?

GIRL: Well, I suppose it's sort of sophisticated.

OLDER LADY: 'Then when he leaves her, she meets a lesbian who
puts her on the street as a "brass nail".'

GIRL: What's a brass nail?

CHAP: Don't ask me, I'm only here for the beer.

BOX MAN: Ha ha dibloody ha ha! Taking the piss out of us little
people again.

(*On the projection screen an image of a shy and beautiful
Edwardian girl. From the loudspeakers the sweet draining
sound of the soprano in Handel's* The Ode to Saint Cecilia's
Day.)

'But oh, what art can teach,
What human voice can reach,
The sacred organ's praise.'

CHAIRMAN:
'Now we maun totter down, John,
And hand in hand we'll go,
And sleep thegither at the foot, John Anderson, my jo.'

GIRL: 'Men are suspicious; prone to discontent; . . .'

CHAIRMAN: 'Subjects still loathe the present Government.'

GRANDFATHER:
'This is the time of day when the weight of bedclothes
Is harder to bear than a sharp incision of steel.
The endless anonymous croak of a cheap transistor

Intensifies the lonely terror I feel.'

(*The* CHAP *goes over to his* FATHER *at the piano.*)

CHAP (*gently*): Come and sit down. It's all over for *you*.

GRANDFATHER: Well, it was all over for him thirty years ago.

FATHER (*allowing himself to be led to a chair*): I am as old as the century.

GIRL: So you say.

OLDER LADY (*reading*): 'Number 53. Did you ever fancy getting hold of a pretty young girl-scout and fucking her up the arse-hole? Well, the two lucky lads in this picture story did just that. You see this lovely young girl was canvassing through their apartment block while they were in the process of screwing this girl, from both front and back. Well, when the girl-scout rang their bell they got the girl to get dressed and coax her in; once they got her inside they stripped her and gave her such a fucking she'll never forget it. Both of them get up her tiny little arse-hole. GREAT.'

(*On the projection screen, a scene from the final ensemble of* Der Rosenkavalier, *the sweeping melody for the* Marschallin, *and so on*)

'Hab mirs gelobt, ihn lieb—zu haben.'

CHAIRMAN:

'She is a winsome wee thing,
She is a handsome wee thing,
She is a lo'esome wee thing.
This sweet wee wife of mine.'

BOX MAN: Nancy Gobble Job, you mean!

GIRL (*to the* CHAP):

'Give me a kiss, and to that kiss a score;
Then to that twenty, add a hundred more:
A thousand to that hundred: so kiss on,
To make that thousand up a million.
Treble that million, and when that is done,
Let's kiss afresh, as when we first begun.'

CHAP: Oh, shut up, you silly bitch.

OLDER LADY (*reading*): 'A picture story of hard rape! Six men drinking in a small bar in Germany decide to grab the pretty little blonde barmaid and have a giggle with her but, as many things do, it went wrong. She resisted! They ganged up on her and tore her clothes off of her and proceeded to violate her in every way that they could. Each one had a go at fucking her, some in her bum, some in her mouth. They held her on the table and screwed until she finally passed out from the spunk forced down her throat. I have seen some rape scenes while I have been in this business, but *WOW*.'

CHAIRMAN: 'Tho' poor in gear, we're rich in love.'

CHAP:

'Bid me to live, and I will live
Thy Protestant to be: . . .'

BOX MAN: Watch it, you've got some of your bleeding Catholics out here!

CHAIRMAN: Just ignore him.

CHAP:

'Or bid me love, and I will give
A loving heart to thee.
A heart as soft, a heart as kind,
A heart as sound and free
As in the whole world thou canst find,
That heart I'll give to thee.'

GIRL:

'My true love hath my heart and I have his,
By just exchange one for the other giv'n;
I hold his dear, and mine he cannot miss,
There never was a better bargain driv'n.'

GRANDFATHER:

' "O words are lightly spoken"
Said Pearse to Connolly,
"Maybe a breath of politic words
Has withered our Rose Tree;
Or maybe but a wind that blows
Across the bitter sea." '

OLDER LADY: 'Homo Action No. 5. As the cover picture shows we have found a young man who is double jointed enough to suck his own cock whilst he is being fucked by a big prick.' (*On the projection screen a large rose.*)

141

CHAIRMAN: I suppose they'll play something from 'Cosi fan Tutte' now.

(*Naturally, the loudspeakers do.*)

GIRL: Of course.

CHAIRMAN: Well, I'll say this bit about the Rose anyway, and get it over with.

(*Fade music.*)

'And my fause lover stole my rose
But ah! he left the thorn wi' me.'

CHAP: Or, as he'd have said himself:

'Don't let the awkward squad fire over me.'

GRANDFATHER: I suppose it's all right. It seems a bit sad.

CHAP: Well at least you can't frighten the horses any longer.

OLDER LADY (*reading*): 'Free offer. Two young teen-age Sea Scouts are in the apartment of randy man; they were collecting for charity but they collected more than they bargained for. It didn't take him long to get their panties down and his big prick into their young mouths and cunts. Second No. 3. An efficiency expert comes into a humdrum office to get it running smoothly, then he gets the old maidenly book-keeper in and shows her how to fuck, when he gets them all at it he leaves. VERY FUNNY AND GOOD!'

(*The* FATHER *begins to play and* GRANDFATHER *stands up and sings.*)

GRANDFATHER:

'Life like an ever-rolling stream
Bears all its sons away.
They fly forgotten as a dream. . .'

(*All join in including* BOX MAN.)

ALL: 'Dies at the opening day.'

BOX MAN (*applauding himself as much as anybody*): That's a good one, that is.

INTERRUPTER: It's still filth and it always was.

(*Note: During the singing of the Hymn by the* GRANDFATHER *the projection screen shows an enormous ascending jet plane with the words 'If you want to get away, jet away'.*)

OLDER LADY: ' "Panther Kidnap." Two young members of the Black Panthers kidnap a white girl on the street and take her back to their pad. There they tear her clothes from her and make her perform all sorts of sexual perversions. She tries to fight them off but these two blacks are much too powerful for her. Lots of good action.'

(*The* FATHER *does another Jack Buchanan and sings a few bars of* Two Little Bluebirds.)

GIRL 'I dare not ask a kiss;
    I dare not beg a smile;
    Lest having that, or this,
    I might grow proud the while.

    No, no, the utmost share,
    Of my desire shall be
    Only to kiss that air,
    That lately kissed thee.'

CHAIRMAN:
    'Doubt you to whom my Muse these notes intendeth,
    Which now to my breast o'ercharged to music lendeth?
    To you, to you, all song of praises due;
    Only in you my song begins and endeth.'

GIRL: 'Thy fair heart my heart enchained.'

CHAP: ' "Fool!" said my Muse, to me, "Look in thy heart and write." '

(*The stage lights dim a little while the loudspeakers play a few bars from* The Lark Ascending.

As the music ends abruptly, so do the lights come up and the OLDER LADY *continues with her next recitative.*)

OLDER LADY (*reading*): ' "Dog Scene." Not wishing to get into trouble with you animal lovers let me state right here, that although this is a very good action film with two girls a man and a dog it is by no means all action with the dog. He does, however, do a very good job of fucking both the girls then the man takes over for the screwing while the dog watches. A GOODY!'

(*On the projection screen a long view of a densely trafficked motorway. On the loudspeakers a few bars of 'Dorabella' from the* Enigma Variations.

Once again the music stops in almost mid bar as the lights snap on.)

GRANDFATHER:

'A man on his own in the car,
Is revenging himself on his wife;
He opens the throttle and bubbles with dottle
And puffs at his pitiful life.

"She's losing her looks very fast,
She loses her temper all day;
That lorry won't let me get past,
This Mini is blocking my way.

Why can't you step on it and shift her!
I can't go on crawling like this!
At breakfast she said that she wished I was dead——
Thank heavens we don't have to kiss.

I'd like a nice blonde on my knee
And one who won't argue or nag.
Who dares to come hooting at *me*?
I only give way to a Jag." '

CHAP:

'Take thou of me smooth pillows, sweetest bed;
A chamber deaf to noise and blind to light,
A rosy garland and a weary head.'

OLDER LADY: "Anal Fuck." If you have ever had a snooty girl
working for YOU, perhaps you have felt like doing to her
what these two bosses did to this girl; after she had
destroyed several hours's hard work, they grabbed her and
tore her clothes off and while one fucked her in her cunt
the other stuck his prick up her arse. A very good film with
excellent colour work.'

(*During the* OLDER LADY'S *gentle declamation appears a fairly
pretty contemporary young girl on the projection screen.
Immediately this is finished, the loudspeakers play a few bars of*
The Nimrod *variation of Elgar. Stop.*)

CHAP:

'Her pretty feet
Like snails did creep
A little out, and then,
As if they started at Bo-Peep,
Did soon draw in agen.'

144

CHAIRMAN:

    'Bid me to weep, and I will weep,
    While I have eyes to see.
    Bid me despair, and I'll despair,
    Under that cypress tree;
    Or bid me die, and I will dare
    E'en Death, to die for thee.'

CHAP:

    'Thou art my life, my love, my heart,
    The very eyes of me:
    And hast command of every part,
    To live and die for thee.'

OLDER LADY (*reading*):

    ' "The Diver." Skindiving enthusiasts will like this approach.
    Two girls bathing on a lonely beach suddenly find that they
    are being observed from beneath by a diver with an aqua-
    lung. He takes off one of the girls' bras and chases her up
    the beach for her pants; the other girl tries to help but she
    is soon stripped as well. Then lots of fucking. GREAT.'
    (*During this sequence,* SKINDIVERS, *male and female, appear on
    the projection screen.*)

BOX MAN: I know where I'm going for *my* holidays next year.

CHAIRMAN: 'That sweet enemy, France.'

CHAP:

    'They love indeed who quake to say they love.
    Oh heav'nly fool, thy most kiss-worthy face
    Anger invests with such lovely grace,
    That Anger's self I needs must kiss again.'

OLD LADY (*reading*): This one's called 'Straight Wife Swap'.
    (*On projection screen lone piper in kilt, possibly Ghurka.
    Plays* The Flowers of the Forest.)

INTERRUPTER (*as lights snap back on*): What's all this thing about
    the Scots?

CHAIRMAN:

    'No! The lough and the mountain, the ruins and rain
    And purple blue distances bound your demesne,
    For the tunes to the elegant measures you trod
    Have chords of deep longing for Ireland and God.'

INTERRUPTER: Is this *ever* going to end?

BOX MAN: Sing us another song!

(*The stage lights darken and on the projection screen a picture of miners emerging from the pit appears. On the loudspeakers is played* Cwm Rhondda.

The entire cast on stage stands with the exception of the GIRL.

However, the BOX MAN *stands up as reverently as he can with a bottle of beer to his lips.*)

INTERRUPTER: Oh, it's the *Welsh* now, is it?

GIRL (*to* BOX MAN): What are you standing up for? You're not even Welsh.

BOX MAN: No, but they're the best rugby players we've got.

CHAIRMAN: Have you ever watched rugby?

BOX MAN: No, have you?

CHAIRMAN: No, but I went to Rugby school.

GIRL: You would.

BOX MAN: Up Chelsea!

OLDER LADY (*reading*): 'A very good yarn about straight sex, lesbianism, feminine domination and flagellation.'

(*On screen, a picture of a young couple kissing one another, somewhat chastely, but with undoubted passion. During this, the* FATHER *plays on the piano and sings.*)

FATHER:

'I like a nice cup of tea in the morning
And a nice cup of tea with my tea,
And at half past eleven
My idea of heaven is a nice cup of tea.'

CHAIRMAN (*singing*):

'And when it's time for bed,
There's a lot to be said
For a nice cup of tea!'

BOX MAN: 'For a nice cup of tea!'

(*He downs some more brown ale.*)

CHAP:

'Leave me, O love, which reacheth but to dust;
And thou, my mind, aspire to higher things;
Grown rich in that which never taketh rust;
Whatever fades, but fading pleasure brings.'

GRANDFATHER: 'Never love was so abused.'

    (*to himself*) I seem to remember that somewhere . . .

GIRL (*to* CHAP):

    'O fair! O sweet! When I do look on thee,
    In whom all joys so well agree, . . .'

CHAP: Lying bitch!

GIRL: Yes!

    'Heart and soul do sing in me,
    Just accord all music makes.'

OLDER LADY (*reading*): ' "The Rustlers" '! This one appears to be, what does it say, oh yes, 'lesbian and straight, this story is about cowboys'.

    (*On the screen a picture of blind and gassed British soldiers from the First World War. The music is* The British Grenadiers. *After the usual harsh snap-out the* GRANDFATHER *rises again and talks almost to himself.*)

GRANDFATHER: It was seven-thirty a.m. on July 1st, 1916. That's when we went over the top.

INTERRUPTER: Yes, we know all that, 'sixty thousand casualties and two for every yard of the front'.

CHAP: Not bad for all that.

GRANDFATHER: More like the end, if you like to say so.

CHAP: Obvious.

CHAIRMAN: True, nonetheless.

BOX MAN: We don't want to hear all about that.

CHAIRMAN: I think that's pretty clear.

FATHER (*sings*):

    'I'm on a see-saw;' 'Room 504,'

OLDER LADY (*reads again*): ' "Slave Girl." Two stories of whipping, spanking and sex.'

GIRL: 'Won't you change partners and dance . . .'

    (*They all sit and listen rather dejectedly to* Variations on a Theme of Thomas Tallis, *at some time during which the* BOX MAN, *in a fit of generosity, starts to throw down bottles of brown ale to the* CHAIRMAN, *who distributes them among the actors and actresses.*)

BOX MAN: Here, have a drink on me.

(*to the audience*) Well, what are you all doing? Just fuck all.
I think they *need* a drink.

INTERRUPTER: *We* need something.

GIRL: We all do.

CHAP: I do . . . If I don't get it soon, I'll go potty.

GRANDFATHER (*to* BOX MAN): Your very good health, sir.

(*All the* ACTORS *on the stage rise and toast the* BOX MAN.)

BOX MAN: Jolly good luck. What about a bit more of that stuff?

CHAP (*sings*):

'They're writing songs of love,
But not for me.'

GIRL (*sings*):

'Every time we say goodbye,
I die a little . . .'

OLDER LADY: Yes, of course. Where are my glasses?

BOX MAN: Someone kindly give this old lady her glasses.

(*The* CHAP *does so.*)

OLDER LADY (*reads*): 'In time with the heaving of her own hips,
Miss Twitch moderately beat the youth's bottom. The
movement of her body increased——'

GIRL: Well, it would——

OLDER LADY: '——increased in its intensity with the strapping until
she stiffened and sighed.' I think *this* one's rather dull. It just
says 'Two Stories of whipping, spanking and sex.'

BOX MAN: Nothing wrong with that. Takes all sorts, you know.

CHAIRMAN (*leaning over to* OLDER LADY): May I have a quick
butchers?

OLDER LADY: Of course. My eyes are getting tired anyway.

GIRL: I was just hoping he wouldn't use rhyming slang. It's so
fatiguing to listen to.

(CHAIRMAN *reads from the piece of paper.*)

CHAIRMAN (*reading*): ' "To Each His Own. He paused, waiting,
and—sure enough, as with his finger Robin's bottom
accepted this new degree of dilation; and the lad relaxed—
so that he could thrust again—and force half the length . . .
Another gasp and a temporary tensing resulted from this
thrust—but this sudden clenching of Robin's rectum only
added to the thrills that David was getting from the opening

148

of this virginal bottom." *HOMOSEXUAL WITH A TINY BIT OF 'BI'.'*

INTERRUPTER: Some of us, you know, did go out at the time and try and do something about all that and it did get done, like it or not.

OX MAN: Quite right.

HAP: Some of your best friends are pouves.

INTERRUPTER: And it ill behoves——

GIRL: I do like 'it ill behoves'.

HAP: Not bad.

GIRL (*to* INTERRUPTER): Shut up, revue artist.

HAP: Bullshit artist.

    'Too long a sacrifice
    Can make a stone of the heart.
    O when may it suffice?
    That is Heaven's part, our part
    To murmur name upon name——'

GRANDFATHER:

    'They must to keep their certainty accuse
    All that are different of a base intent;
    Pull down established honour; hawk for news
    Whatever their loose fantasy invent
    And murmured with bated breath, as though
    The abounding gutter had been Helicon
    Or calumny a song.   How can they know
    Truth flourishes where the student's lamp has shone,
    And there alone, that have no solitude?
    So the crowd come they care not what may come.
    They have loud music, hope every day renewed
    And heartier loves; that lamp is from the tomb.'

CHAIRMAN: I think we're mostly agreed about that.

INTERRUPTER: We most certainly are not.

OX MAN: Give him another drink.

    (*He throws down another bottle of beer to the* CHAIRMAN *who does his best to catch it skilfully.*)

CHAIRMAN: Thank you.

    (*As he drinks from the bottle, the Union Jack appears on the screen and the loudest, most rousing version is heard of Blake's* Jerusalem.)

INTERRUPTER: Oh God!

    (*He groans and moves off to the bar. The music snaps off
    again and the* CHAIRMAN *addresses the audience.*)

CHAIRMAN: Well, it's a sort of agreement.

    'No, no, not night but death;
    Was it needless death after all?'

CHAP: Cheers.

BOX MAN: God bless you. Is that *poetry*? Or just *talking*?

CHAIRMAN: Just talking.

    'For England may keep faith
    For all that is done and said.'

BOX MAN: Don't you worry. I *said* it was the World Cup this time.
And I'll take on anybody!

CHAIRMAN:

    'We know their dream; enough
    To know they dreamed and are dead;
    And what if excess of love
    Bewildered them till they died?'

CHAP: Just a minute before you sit down.

    (*He hails the* STAGE MANAGER *and he and the* CHAIRMAN
    help to wheel on a pulpit. As they do so, the panatrope plays
    the Prisoners' song 'Durch Nacht Zum Licht' from Fidelio. As
    soon as the pulpit is in place, the music stops, the* STAGE
    MANAGER *goes off and the* CHAP *addresses the* GIRL.)

CHAP: You, I think.

GIRL: Oh no, you. I can't do imitations.

CHAP: Well, you *can*, actually. Impressions, really.
Which are much better. However——

    (*He ascends the pulpit and addresses the theatre in a thick
    Belfast accent. As he does so, the projection screen shows a
    group of extremely tough looking British troops in flak kit
    and riot masks, etc., facing a crowd of Irish civilians. L.C.*)

And I say to you, the British people, and by that I mean
the people of Northern Ireland, that not only myself but all
decent proper-thinking people throughout the world,
whether Protestant or Catholic, are shocked daily and
troubled by the tragic sight of our troops who must be the
best, as well as the most disciplined in the world, being

incited physically, to say nothing of them morally and
spiritually, of seeing them, having to stand inactive
behind their shields while a lot of ignorant thugs
and hooligans are pelting at them with their bombs and
guns!

INTERRUPTER: There should be an Independent Inquiry.

BOX MAN: Quite right. Bloody hooligans.

GIRL (*turning on audience*): Murdering British soldiers, they're all
bloody murderers! You're all bloody murderers.

BOX MAN: Why don't you get back to Ireland and let us
unemployed British get on with the job!?

GIRL: Who needs England?

BOX MAN: *You* do for a start.

CHAP (*descending from the pulpit*): Right. Someone else carry on.
I was running out of steam anyway.

GIRL: That was clear.

(*The* CHAP *assists the* GIRL *into the pulpit. During this, the
Irish tricolour waves on the screen to an appropriate Gallic
tune. The* GIRL *addresses the audience from the pulpit.*)

GIRL: You all know what I think——

BOX MAN: I should say we do, we've heard it enough times.

GIRL: Well, it needs repeating to get into concrete skulls like
yours. Get out of Ireland!

BOX MAN: Get out of England!

GIRL: Don't think I won't!

BOX MAN: Good!

GIRL: You've oppressed us for three centuries.

BOX MAN: What about it? Bloody idle lot. Think you're all poets
and dreamers, I know. Shall I tell you something, mate?
The only thing that ever came out of Ireland——

GIRL: I know, is horses and writers.

BOX MAN: And who said that?

GIRL: A lot of Horse Protestants. And I'll bet you didn't know
who said that.

BOX MAN: Some bloody Catholic I.R.A. man.

GIRL: You're damn right.

BOX MAN: Well, I bet he did a damn sight better in London than
in Dublin.

GIRL: You're right——

BOX MAN: Do you want a brown ale? Of course I suppose you only drink bleeding Guinness.

GIRL: Stick your brown ale.

BOX MAN: And you stick your Guinness, and I hope——

GIRL: 'The ship goes down in Galway Bay.' That's the way with the lot of you.

CHAIRMAN: Oh dear, would anyone else like to say something?

INTERRUPTER: Yes.

BOX MAN: Shut your gob.

CHAIRMAN: Well, we do at least know that *that's* an Irish expression.

INTERRUPTER: I think it's all very well——

BOX MAN: Taking the piss out of the Irish——

INTERRUPTER: If you like. But what I object to, and I don't just say this on behalf of my wife——

GIRL (*descending from pulpit*): You wouldn't.

INTERRUPTER: But, as I was going to say before you interrupted me, all these jibes about bigotry are all very well but personally I find the implicit condescension inherent——

CHAP: Inherent!

INTERRUPTER: Yes, sir, inherent. It's a perfectly proper word and expresses what I mean to say.

CHAP: Which is——?

INTERRUPTER: That using a woman——

CHAP: As an object? Or were you going to say stereotype?

INTERRUPTER: Simply that you are being snide and coarse at the expense of a great many highly able and misused women. Fortunately, you will no longer be able to get away with it.

CHAP: I didn't think I *had* got away with it. Perhaps I didn't try hard enough.

OLDER LADY: I quite agree with that gentleman. He is rather bad-mannered and silly, but, in this case, I think he's quite right. (*to the* CHAIRMAN): May I say a few words?

CHAIRMAN: By all means do. *You'll* probably say something sensible.

OLDER LADY: Thank you. (*She has already ascended the pulpit.*) May I say first that I have no particular personal complaint. In some ways, I was born into a good time.

And because of my natural intelligence, have managed to cope with what to most *men* would be an intolerable situation. My young friend here has complained, if I heard him correctly, of one of his earlier girlfriends being sick in the grounds of Norwich Cathedral. However, I would just say to him and others like him that it is a mere fact of life that women at all times and at all ages have suffered from, and in many cases died from, not merely childbirth but from what you would no doubt call the inbuilt tedium of organs such as the cervix, the vulvae, the vagina and the womb.

BOX MAN: Disgusting.

OLDER LADY: If men had to undergo what they so cheerfully call 'the curse'——

BOX MAN: Period pains——

OLDER LADY: ——They would have long ago invented some alleviation.

BOX MAN: Invent it yourself. Sing us a song.

OLDER LADY: I'm afraid our young friend here has let him delude himself into dreaming about something he thinks of as 'Eternal Woman'.

BOX MAN: Who doesn't?

OLDER LADY: That is because she is only valued by the excitement she may or may not arouse.

BOX MAN: Get off out of it, you old bag.

OLDER LADY: In short, she has to be desirable.

BOX MAN: Well, it does help, lady.

OLDER LADY: In the case of men, it appears not to be necessary. We women can be put down, if that is the expression, by the flimsiest physical or intellectual failing. We have been eternally abandoned from the Old Testament onwards. All I say to you now is that we may all probably totally abandon you. Men, I mean.

(*She turns to the* CHAP, *who applauds.*)

OLDER LADY: Would you mind?

CHAP: Certainly.

(*He assists her down the steps although she seems to be in no real need of it.*)
My turn.

CHAIRMAN: Hurry it up a bit.

CHAP: Right ho, squire.

The nude is female by definition. Nudity is evasive, fleeing from description, allusive . . .

(*During this speech, various classic female nudes appear on the screen.*)

The naked male may be powerful, even beautiful, but self-defining like a jet aircraft in flight. Seldom is it more than technology made Flesh. Female, in this sense, is Art. The Male is Critic. Or, so it seems to me at this moment. Female is Art, secretive even when it conceals nothing. Revealing all, it is no sphinx for nothing, it contains and sustains life itself, taming random seed and even time. Making mystery of woman, the liberationists would say, is to belittle her in a glib religious conspiracy of fake mystery. Imprison her with the useful poetry of femininity and you destroy her in a cloud of voracious male imagination and inevitable social enslavement. The course of history! Woman is dead! Long live Woman! . . .

I do not believe it. She has always triumphed in *my* small corner of spirit, just as I have failed *her* image—my broken, misty, self-deceiving image you may say—during most of my life. And, remembering it, what a long time it has been. I believe in Woman, whatever that may be, just as I believe in God, because they were both invented by man. If I am their inventor, they are my creators, and they will continue to exist. During most of my life. What made me think of it? Watching a couple in a street late at night in a provincial town. Being in love, how many times and over such a period. Being in Love! What anathema to the Sexual Militant, the wicked interest on free capital.

Anathema because it involves waste, exploitation of resources, sacrifice, unplanned expenditure, both sides sitting down together in unequal desolation. *This* is the market place I have known and wandered in almost as long as I indecently remember or came to forget. Being in love, quaint expense of spirit, long over-ripe for the bulldozer; of negotiating from the strength of unmanning women's liberation. Those long-shore bullies with bale hooks in bras and trousers seamed with slogans and demands . . . Being in love. Desolation in the sea of hope itself. Sentimental? False? Infantile? Possibly. And infantile because my memories of the phenomenon, if there be such a one, is or ever will be, start so *young*. From three, yes, I know it was three, even till the only twenty-one, there were so many girls, girl-women, women of all ages, I loved. Very few of them were in love with me, alas. Being in love blunders all negotiations and certainly differentials. I have been sometimes indecently moved to tears and if there were a court of justice in these things, I would have been dealt with summarily as a persistent offender, asking for innumerable, nameless and unspeakable offences to be taken into account. However, if I have been such a villain in this manner of feelings, I have tried to be as clever as I know how. Knowing, as we all know, that there is no such thing. If I have used blunt instruments and sophisticated gear, I've tried to avoid soft risks and only go for the big stuff. Naturally, I've made mistakes. In fact, when you look at it, the successful jobs have been far fewer than the fair cops. But that is the nature of crime itself, of *being in love*; you are incapable of adding up the obvious odds against you, unlike the law abider with his common sense and ability to discriminate between his own needs and that of the rest of society. To sustain and endure beneath the law——

GIRL: *Beneath*, naturally——

CHAP: ——Being in love is a crime against women, and yes, oh yes, reducing them to objects—as this splendid lady has pointed out. To fantasies of poetry, poetry and piety and bourgeois poetry, notwithstanding the workers at that. It demeans men and serves their historic despotism, whatever you think, over the female. So much is said; so let it *be* so. It has not been the truth to *my* past; though it may well be that of one who has been a truly conniving peasant toiling under vicious and unnerving tyranny. The revolution is about to break, comrades, and I for one shall not wait to be explainable or force heads down in the opening wave

of forced collective. *Girls past.* If I ever yearned for a
figment England, so I yearned for *them*; for girls past, fewer
in the present and sadly, probably in the future. Who *were*
they? All I remember most is their names, what they wore,
sometimes what they looked like. Not very much.

GIRL: You've said that about four hundred times.

CHAP: So I have. Yes. I have indeed . . .

(*He descends from the pulpit and he and the* GIRL *clasp each
other.*)

GIRL: Heart of my heart . . .

CHAP: Heart of *my* heart . . .

GIRL: People don't fall in love.

(*to audience*)

That idea is no longer effective in the context of modern
techniques. We are not nations or nation states. All that
must go. We are part of an efficient, maximum productive
ECONOMIC UNION. And Economic Unions do not fall in love.
They amalgamate. They cut down. They are NOW in the
Land's future. We are that Land and we are on the brink
of Progress. Even Progress has its cliché programmer.
But there. We have nothing but gain to contemplate. Loss,
such as it may have been, is, has been, ground into the
shining, kindly present even that is *ours* already! Even at
this moment. We are tearing down. We build! We build
now. And NOW.

We are not language. We are lingua. We do not love, eat
or cherish. We *exchange*. Oh yes: we talk. We have words,
rather: environment; pollution; problems; *issues*; oh, and——.
So century, century as is and will be—APPROCHE MOI!
Approche moi. To me . . .

(*The* GIRL *turns from the audience and kisses the* CHAP.)

CHAP: Oh, heart, dearest heart. What does *that* mean! Rhetoric.
I do, I have, I've wanted you, want you, will, *may* not and
so on. I love you, yes. I shall. Shan't. Heart . . . And I want,
yes—here we go—want to fuck you . . . Not cum-uppance
or any of that . . . Heart: I want you. Legs high. High.
Open. Prone: if you like. We can both laugh. And enjoy.
Enjoy me if you can. I *do* enjoy you. I *do*. I want you,

thighs enveloping my head. Mist. I shall want to breathe . . .
Give me *you*. I'll do what I can with me. I hate to use the
words between us—but—I want what I know, have known,
we know has taken, done, enjoyed, laughed over;
cherished. Between us. Girl. Chap. We are lost without . . '.
You *know*. Don't you?

GIRL: Yes. I really think—perhaps—I do.

CHAP: Do. Don't. Will. Won't. Can. Can't. I wish I were *inside*
you. Now. At this moment . . . However.

GIRL: So do I. *However* . . .

BOX MAN: Very nicely expressed.

CHAIRMAN: What do you know about it?

BOX MAN: If I may be allowed to say so.

(*Everyone in the cast looks up at the* BOX MAN, *with the exception
of the* GIRL *and the* CHAP *who are intent upon each other*.)

CAST: Piss off.

CHAIRMAN: (*sings to the* FATHER'S *accompaniment*) My balls are
like a red, red rose.

BOX MAN: What time is it, for Christ's sake?

GIRL (*to the* CHAP): I've watched for you all my life.

CHAP: Likewise.

GIRL: And looked and wanted and as you would say, observed.

(BOX MAN *stands up and sings the opening bars of a patriotic
song. The auditorium is then almost bludgeoned by a recording
of the same song. After a few bars of this, the* CHAIRMAN
gets up, holding his bentwood chair.)

CHAIRMAN: Well, I think that'll have to do this time.

CHAP: It will.

CHAIRMAN: I'm not a good chairman at all.

INTERRUPTER: No!

CHAIRMAN: Very well, then——

(*He extends his hands to the rest of the cast and they all stand
hand in hand together and sing* Widdecombe Fair *in its
original. During the song they produce bunting with the words
on each piece* THE—VERY—BEST—OF—BRITISH—LUCK.)

CAST:

'Tom Pearce, Tom Pearce,
Come lend me your grey mare,

All along, down along, out along lea,
For I want to go to Widdecombe Fair
With Peter Davey,
Dan'l Widden . . .'
(*And so on.* CHAIRMAN *addresses the audience.*)
CHAIRMAN: So: that's what you'd call your lot. *Our* lot . . . And
may the Good Lord bless you and keep you. Or God rot
you.
(*All the* CAST *hum* When You Are Weary, Friend of Mine
as they pick up their chairs and go off, leaving the
GRANDFATHER, *who strums and sings* Old Father Thames.
*He then goes off with his chair and the stage lights dim as
one of the stage management comes on and idly turns the
handle of the barrel organ.*
*The cast return to face the audience but with no sense of 'Taking
A Call'. The* INTERRUPTER *boos and walks out, the* BOX MAN
*applauds enthusiastically and drinks some more beer. The actors
go off as the curtain falls.*)